American
Pewter
in the
Museum of Fine Arts
Boston

American
Pewter
in the
Museum of Fine Arts
Boston

Department of American Decorative Arts and Sculpture

Photographs by Daniel Farber

Distributed by NEW YORK GRAPHIC SOCIETY, Greenwich, Connecticut
Published by MUSEUM OF FINE ARTS, BOSTON

Copyright 1974 by
Museum of Fine Arts, Boston
All rights reserved
Library of Congress
Catalogue Card No. 74-78551
SBN 0-87846-080-2
Designed by Carl Zahn
and Barbara Hawley
Typeset by Dumar Typesetting, Inc.,
Dayton, Ohio
Printed by Scroll Press,
Danbury, Connecticut

Front cover and frontispiece:
Table setting of pewter arranged in the
parlor from the Brown-Pearl house,
West Boxford, Massachusetts,
at the Museum of Fine Arts, Boston.

Back cover:
Pewter arranged in the parlor
cupboard from the Brown-Pearl house,
West Boxford, Massachusetts,
at the Museum of Fine Arts, Boston.

Contents

Preface

The collection of American pewter in the Museum of Fine Arts, Boston, is listed here in its entirety. This catalogue is intended to serve as a record of the museum's holdings for comparison with other pewter collections, both public and private. It also serves as an accompaniment to an exhibition at the Museum of Fine Arts honoring the fortieth annual meeting of the Pewter Collectors' Club of America in Boston, May 1974. The finest examples of holloware (pitchers, flagons, tankards, teapots, etc.) are illustrated. Examples of the same type are included in the checklist along with other pieces of little pictorial interest, such as plates, dishes, etc.

The arrangement of the catalogue is by state, from north to south, and by maker, alphabetically within each state. Unidentified and unknown makers follow the known makers. All marks are identified from pieces in the Museum of Fine Arts collection, and every one possible has been photographed (not to scale). When a mark has been identified in Ledlie I. Laughlin, *Pewter in America, Its Makers and Their Marks* (abbreviated to LIL) and Charles F. Montgomery, *A History of American Pewter* (abbreviated to CFM), references to these are given in addition to the photograph of the mark. References are to figure number unless page is indicated. The placement of marks is mentioned for each piece with the exception of plates, dishes, and basins, when it is assumed the mark is on the outside bottom, unless otherwise specified. Dimensions are for overall height and length. Unless otherwise indicated, objects are from the bequest of Mrs. Stephen S. FitzGerald.

Preparation of the catalogue involved many talents. First thanks are due to Mr. William O. Blaney, who encouraged the project and helped to clean the pewter, with the assistance of Nancy Webbe and Eleuthera duPont, who also sorted, measured, typed, and assisted with photographic preparations. Mr. Daniel Farber generously donated talent and materials for all photographs and developed a system of photography that makes pewter look like pewter. Anne Farnam worked on the final manuscript and, with Nancy Webbe and Eleuthera duPont, arranged the exhibition. In technical cleaning of difficult pewter we are grateful for assistance from William Young, Merville Nichols, and members of the Research Laboratory. Never before has the collection been in such good health.

Introduction

Only a few generations ago, our ancestors used pewter daily. Appreciated for its utility and beauty, this bright alloy was found in the ordinary household as well as the aristocratic mansion, in the towns and in the country. Everyday needs were well served by pewter plates, vessels, and candlesticks. Pewter plate and holloware were standard equipment in taverns and churches. Inns had pewter tankards, mugs, beakers, and plates, and the ecclesiastical pewter of the meetinghouse took the form of chalices, communion plates, baptismal bowls, and sometimes elaborate altar candlesticks. The varied forms and uses of pewter in America before the time of the Civil War transcended differences of race, creed, and social class. This broad popular use of pewter in our past captures our imagination today—especially as we seek to identify the arts of the common man. One is tempted to characterize American pewter objects as art of and for the people; it seems a peculiarly democratic art form.[1]

Like that of most of the earliest colonial crafts, the story of pewter is one of slowly changing traditions and rich sources of materials. Materials and methods of production hark back to the craft practices of medieval England.[2] Tin, always the chief metal of the pewter alloy, came from the famous mines of Cornwall, where the abundant ore *cassiterite* was found in solid, broad veins. Large lumps of this ore, bluish white in color streaked with yellow brown, and rocklike in appearance, were hoisted into heaps near the mouths of mine shafts, then broken into smaller pieces and sent off to stamping mills for crushing. From there the ore was taken to furnaces for smelting and molding into tin ingots, or *blocktin,* as it was called.[3]

The best quality pewter ware contained as much as ninety-nine percent pure tin. Varying small proportions of copper, antimony, or bismuth were sometimes added to alter the melting point, add strength, improve casting qualities, or improve ductility. But the alloy with a high concentration of tin was considered the best grade.[4] Tin gave pewter its light color and soft luster. To signify high-grade pewter, or *hard metal,* as it was called in the eighteenth century, the pewterer both in America and in England frequently marked his ware with an X or modified-crowned X. Ordinary plates and mugs were made of second-grade pewter and

1. The story of pewter in America is well told by many writers and collectors. The most recent work is *A History of American Pewter,* by Charles F. Montgomery, Curator of the Garvan and Related Collections of American Art, Yale University. This highly readable book reveals a wealth of facts, historical insights, and an affection for pewter. The most monumental work, *Pewter in America: Its Makers and Their Marks,* written by Ledlie Irwin Laughlin, was first published in 1940 in two volumes; a third volume by the same author was published in 1971. With these two sources (hereafter referred to as Montgomery and Laughlin), the reader can explore the field of American pewter in depth. Additional references are listed in the selected bibliography included in this catalogue.
2. For the English background, see H. H. Cotterell, *Old Pewter, Its Makers and Marks* (London: Batsford, 1929).
3. A brief description of the mines of Cornwall is given by James G. Percival, *The Wonders of the World . . .* (New Haven, 1836), pp. 281-283. Laughlin, vol. 3, pp. 1-3, discusses various meanings of the term *blocktin.*
4. It melted easily and spread under the hammer well (high malleability); it could not be drawn into wire (low ductility).

contained seven or eight percent lead in the alloy. This grade was called *trifle metal*. The lowest grade of pewter, *lay metal,* contained sizable quantities of lead and was used for wine measures and chamber pots.[5]

American pewterers employed a high percentage of tin in their ware, as recent laboratory analysis of American pewter reveals.[6] While further research is needed in surveying a broad range of American pewter to detect possible deviations, it seems probable that the American pewterer maintained fairly close control of his alloy in order to successfully compete with ware imported from England. Importation of finished English pewter must have helped to maintain standards in this country and also supplied the colonial pewterer with a continual replenishment of raw material as plates became damaged and worn. Estimates of pewter importation from England are staggering. By the 1760's, the annual importation amounted to more than three hundred tons. Some of this ware was probably destined for the shop windows of the pewter craftsman-merchant, but customers also ordered directly from London, as did John Hancock in 1783. Hancock reportedly liked pewter because "the contents of the plates were not so apt to slide off" and "the use of them caused no clatter in contact with knives and forks."[7]

Pewter making was big business both in England and colonial America. In England, the industry was protected by law, which levied prohibitively high duty on the exportation of raw tin. The colonies, according to English mercantile theory, were a fine burgeoning market for the consumption of manufactured goods from the mother country.

But then, as now, industry cannot be well regulated by law. Pewterers emigrated to this country as early as the seventeenth century and set up trade with evident success. There was plenty of old pewter to refashion into new forms. Worn and damaged pewter could be purchased in America even more cheaply than raw tin in England. The opportunity to sell without a middleman or without strict controls on profits offered much attraction to the pewter craftsman. Henry Shrimpton, after twenty-seven years as a pewterer, brazier, and eventually merchant in Boston, died in 1666 a wealthy man.[8]

The rarity of American pewter dating from the first period of settlement results from wear and the common practice of recasting old pewter into new. One magnificent English charger now in the collection of the Museum of Fine Arts (fig. 1), which survives from the seventeenth century, is probably the earliest known example of pewter with an American history. It was owned by William and Jane Collier, said to have been the richest inhabitants of the Plymouth colony. According to tradition, they brought the charger with them from England when they

5. Montgomery, p. 28.
6. Ibid., pp. 235-239.
7. Montgomery, p. 13, citing Abram E. Brown, *John Hancock, His Book* (Boston, 1898), p. 240.
8. Montgomery, p. 22, cites records of Suffolk County, which show Shrimpton's assets at his death amounted to the considerable sum of £2,000. An enormous quantity of pewter, tools, and other goods owned by Shrimpton are discussed by Montgomery. For additional insight into the conduct of the pewter trade and sales over the counter or through peddlers, see Laughlin, vol. 2, pp. 17-18.

Fig. 1. Charger
English, 17th century
Owner's initials "w^CI" stamped on
rim. H. 1⅜ in., D. of rim 21⅜ in.,
W. of rim 3½ in.
Bequest of Mrs. Andrew W. Laurie.
47.1559
Mark:

Fig. 2. A bill head for Roswell
Gleason & Sons, Dorchester,
Massachusetts

settled in Plymouth in 1633.[9] On the broad rim of the nearly twenty-two-inch charger are stamped the initials "w C i."

In this country almost up to the first decade of the nineteenth century, pewter was made by relatively uncomplicated craft methods. The necessary tools were few: a pewterer could set up a shop with furnace, pots, molds, lathe, anvil, hammers, files, scrapers, and workbench. Pewter was formed by pouring the molten alloy into smoked and heated bronze molds. After knocking the pewter from its mold, edges were trimmed and the surface scraped, skinned, or peeled away on the lathe, and the metal polished.[10] Pewter made by this method was necessarily heavy bodied and durable. The surface of the metal was strong and could endure casual handling without serious damage. Early pewter had the appearance of compactness, utility, simplicity, and strength. Form and surface conveyed the whole artistic message.[11] Because this ware was multiplied time after time from molds, old forms were retained and reused long after styles had changed in the centers of fashion.

In the early years of the nineteenth century, the materials and methods of the pewter craftsman in this country were dramatically transformed. In competition with the sale of glass, pottery, and porcelain, pewter manufacturers experienced a falling off of business. To recapture trade and to increase efficiency of production, pewterers altered their alloy by adding more antimony and changed their forms by working rolled sheets. The following contemporary description of the new process shows how complicated and technical the craft became:

First, the ingredients, tin, antimony, copper, &c., are melted and mixed, then cast into bars. These are reduced to a proper thickness by being passed between two steel rollers, which are adjusted so as to diminish the space at each passage. To make the metal very "quick" and pure, it is then re-melted, re-cast, and re-rolled. It is then cut into circular plates of proper size for the article to be made. These plates are placed over a hollow casting, and pressed into the same by a reverse casting made to fit the opening cavity, thus turning the metal plate into the form of a circular basin, of a size depending upon the size of the plate. This basin, so to speak, is placed in a lathe by the side of a wooden block of the pattern desired, (called a chuck,*) and by pressure against it with a smooth instrument, during the revolution, is brought against the surface of the "chuck" in the form desired. This is called "spinning" and it is by this process that most plain ware is made, the flat piece of metal being converted into the body of a teapot, an urn, or other article. After being spun, it is turned with a sharp tool both inside and out. To turn the inside, it is placed within a hollow "chuck," by which it is held in place and its form preserved.*

It remains now to furnish the vessel with the appropriate trimmings, to wit:

9. According to C. F. Montgomery (correspondence, March 21, 1974) even in England, 1633 is a very early date for a surviving pewter plate.
10. A more thorough discussion of pewter making is given by both Laughlin and Montgomery.
11. Insight into the significance of surface in colonial or provincial art is offered by George Kubler, "Time's Perfection and Colonial Art," an introduction to the 1968 *Winterthur Conference Report* (Winterthur, Delaware, 1969), pp. 7-12.

spout, feet, top, handle, &c. The top may be spun, but the spout, tips, handles, and feet, are cast bright from the melted metal.[12]

The new process released the craftsman from the limitations of form imposed by the bronze molds and resulted in an elaboration of forms. The body and surface of the metal also changed. The new, bright ware, called "Britannia," was no longer heavy bodied and strong. It was considered a major improvement by the trade and was valued by society for its ornamental quality rather than its utility. (Compare catalogue nos. 7 and 216 for examples of Britannia and the earlier pewter.)[13]

The 1870's marked the disappearance of the pewterer's and Britannia maker's trade and the growing popular demand for the more expensive-looking silver plated ware. A bill head of this time for Roswell Gleason & Sons of Dorchester, Massachusetts, shows that silver plate had already taken the place of pewter in this manufacturer's wares (fig. 2).[14]

The American pewter in the Museum of Fine Arts, Boston, dates from the mid-eighteenth century to the third quarter of the nineteenth century. Most of the pieces came to the museum in 1964 as a gift with other works of art from the late Mrs. Stephen S. FitzGerald of Weston, Massachusetts, who had been an active member of the Pewter Collectors' Club. Much of Mrs. FitzGerald's collection was formed in the 1930's. Correspondence from that time shows a host of friendships among the closely linked members of the pewter collecting world. As early as 1938 large plates from Mrs. FitzGerald's collection—works by Samuel and Joseph Danforth, Thomas Badger, Samuel Hamlin, and William Billings—were lent to an exhibition at the Old Dartmouth Historical Society. And from that date her generosity and interest extended to other institutions. Parts of her collection are now in the Metropolitan Museum of Art and in the Connecticut Valley Historical Museum,

12. Description by T. H. Bowman quoted by Edwin T. Freedley, *Leading Pursuits and Leading Men* (Philadelphia: Edward Young, 1856), pp. 404-405. According to Freedley, Bowman was a gentleman who had interest in the Albany Britannia and Excelsior Plating Works established in 1847 by Messrs. Sheldon, Feltman and Wilder. Freedley also discusses the works of T. D. & S. Boardman of Hartford, Connecticut; Hall & Boardman of Philadelphia; Isaac Babbitt's Britannia works in Taunton, Massachusetts; Reed & Barton; The Taunton Britannia and Plate Company; and John H. Whitlock & Co. of Troy, New York.
13. Many handsome objects made by Britannia manufacturers are illustrated in this catalogue. For a detailed account of this ware, see Nancy A. Goyne, "Britannia in America: The Introduction of a New Alloy and a New Industry," *Winterthur Portfolio* 2 (Winterthur, Delaware: The H. F. du Pont Winterthur Museum, 1965), pp. 160-196.
14. Scientific analysis of a silver plated bowl by Roswell Gleason (cat. no. 59) shows the components to be as follows:

	Inside Alloy, %	*Outside Plate, %*
Silver	87.4	91.6
Chromium	.77	.63
Nickel	2.74	2.22
Copper	4.72	2.51
Zinc	1.62	.92
Lead	2.80	.95
Mercury	0	1.2

Springfield, Massachusetts. Through interest of a former staff member, Richard Randall, Jr., the majority of Mrs. FitzGerald's collection came to the Boston Museum.

Like most collections of American pewter in public museums, our collection came about through gifts or bequests from enthusiastic individuals who prized this metal; it reflects the good judgment of those who discovered fine works and had the impulse to share them with others.[15]

JONATHAN FAIRBANKS
Curator

15. Other important pewter collections, privately formed but in public museums, are listed by Montgomery, p. 230.

Catalogue

Maine

Rufus Dunham
1815 - ca. 1882
Westbrook, Maine, active
1837-1860
Mark refs.: A. LIL,vol. 2, p. 100.
B. LIL, vol. 2, p. 100; CFM, 221.
Marks:
A

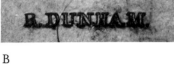

B

Rufus Dunham
3. Teapot
Mark: B, outside bottom. H. 8⅜ in.
64.1772

Rufus Dunham
4. Water pitcher
Mark: A, outside bottom. H. 8½ in.
64.1806

Rufus Dunham
1. Flagon with spout
Mark: A, outside bottom. H. 8⅜
in., D. of rim 5⅜ in., D. of base
6⅝ in.
Gift of the Congregational Church,
Greenland, New Hampshire.
12.1525

3
4

Allen Porter

Westbrook, Maine, active
1830-1840
Mark ref.: A. LIL, vol. 2, p. 109.
Mark:
A

Allen Porter
6. Teapot
Mark: A, outside bottom.
H. 10⅝ in.
64.1783

Freeman Porter

b. 1808

Westbrook, Maine, active
1835-1865
Mark refs.: A. LIL, vol. 2, p. 110;
CFM, p. 226.
Mark:
A

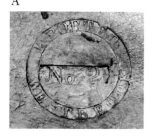

Freeman Porter
9. Teapot
Mark: A, outside bottom. H. 6⅜ in.
64.1780

Freeman Porter
7. Teapot
Mark: A, outside bottom.
H. 10¾ in.
64.1782

6

9

Vermont

Richard Lee, Sr.
1747-1823
Grafton, New Hampshire, 1788-
1790; Ashfield, Massachusetts,
1791-1793; Lanesborough,
Massachusetts, 1794-1802;
Springfield, Vermont, 1802-1820
or
Richard Lee, Jr.
b. 1775
Springfield, Vermont, active
1795-1816
Mark refs.: A. LIL, vol. 1, 410;
CFM, p. 224.
Mark:
A

Richard Lee, Sr. or Jr.
10. Porringer
Mark: A, handle top. H. 1⅛ in.,
D. of rim 3¾ in.
64.1758

10

6

Massachusetts

Nathaniel Austin
1741-1816
Charlestown, Massachusetts,
active 1763-1807
Mark refs.; A. LIL, vol. 1, 296;
CFM, p. 215. B. LIL, vol. 1, 301;
CFM, p. 215. C. LIL, vol 1, 299a;
CFM, p. 215. D. LIL, vol. 1, 300.
Marks:

A

B

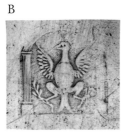

C

D

11

Nathaniel Austin
11. Quart pot
Mark: A, on terminal. H. 5¾ in.,
D. of rim 3⅞ in., D. of base 4⅞ in.
Gift of Francis H. Bigelow. 17.171

Richard Austin
1764-1817
Boston, Massachusetts, active
1793-1807
Mark refs.: A. LIL, vol. 1, 305;
CFM, p. 215. B. LIL, vol. 1, 306.
Marks:

A

B

Richard Austin
20. Basin
Mark: B, inside bottom. H. 1⅞ in.,
D. of rim 8 in., W. of rim ⅜ in.
64.1691

Thomas Badger
1764-1826
Boston, Massachusetts, active
1787-1815
Mark refs.: A. LIL, vol. 1, 309;
CFM, p. 215. B. LIL, vol. 1, 287b;
CFM, p. 215. C. LIL, vol. 1, 308;
CFM, p. 215.
Marks:

A

B

C

Thomas Badger
29. Basin
Mark: A, inside bottom. H. 1⅞ in.,
D. of rim 8⅛ in., W. of rim ⅜ in.
64.2324

20

29

Roswell Gleason
1799-1887
Dorchester, Massachusetts,
active 1821-1871
Mark refs.: A. LIL, vol. 2, p. 102.
B. LIL, vol. 2, p. 102; CFM, p. 222.
Marks:
A

B

ROSWELL GLEASON

Roswell Gleason
45. Teapot
Mark: A, outside bottom. H. 7¾ in.
64.1773

Roswell Gleason (attributed to)
46. Miniature tea set
Mark: none. Teapot: H. 3⅛ in.;
sugar bowl: H. 2 in.; slop basin:
H. 1⅞ in.; cream pot: H. 2⅜ in.;
teacup with saucer: H. ⅞ in.
Anonymous gift. Res. 28.71

45

46

40

Roswell Gleason
40. Coffee urn and drip pan
Mark: Coffee urn, B, outside
bottom. H. 13⅝ in.
Mark: Drip pan, A, outside bottom.
H. 2⅜ in., D. of rim 6 in.
64.1867, 64.1873

47

43

42

Roswell Gleason
47. Bedpan
Mark: B, outside bottom. D. of
rim 11 in.
64.1877

Roswell Gleason
42. Pair of candlesticks
with inserts
Mark: A, outside bottom. H. 4¾ in.
64.1813 a, b; 64.1814 a, b

Roswell Gleason
43. Candlestick (one of a pair)
Mark: A, outside bottom. H. 7 in.
64.1812

11

Roswell Gleason
41. Handled beaker, silvered
Mark: A, outside bottom. H. 4⅜
in., D. of rim 3⅜ in., D. of base
3⅜ in.
64.2349

Roswell Gleason
50. Teapot
Mark: A, outside bottom. H. 9⅞ ir
64.1774

Roswell Gleason
48. Water pitcher
Mark: B, outside bottom. H. 12 in.
64.1807

41

50

12

Samuel Green

ca. 1757 - ca. 1834
Boston, Massachusetts, active
ca. 1794 - 1834
Mark ref.: A. LIL, vol. 1, 302.
Mark:
A

Samuel Green
60. Basin
Mark: A, inside bottom. H. 1¾ in.,
D. of rim 7⅝ in., W. of rim ½ in.
Gift of Mrs. Edward M. Pickman.
63.1047

60

62

David B. Morey
&
R. H. Ober

Boston, Massachusetts, active
1852 - 1855
Mark ref.: A. LIL, vol. 2, p. 107.
Mark:
A

David B. Morey & R. H. Ober
62. Handled beaker
Mark: A, outside bottom. H. 3⅜
in., D. of rim 2⅛ in., D. of base
2¾ in.
64.1727

James H. Putnam
1803-1855
Malden, Massachusetts, active
1830-1855
Mark refs.: A. LIL, vol. 2, p. 110;
CFM, p. 226.
Mark:
A

James H. Putnam
70. Teapot
Mark: A, outside bottom. H. 7⅞ in.
64.1787

James H. Putnam
72. Syrup jug
Mark: A, outside bottom. H. 4⅝ in.
64.1804

70
72

James H. Putnam
71. Teapot
Mark: A, outside bottom. H. 8 in.
64.2366

71

George Richardson

1782-1848

Boston, Massachusetts, active
1818-1828
Cranston, Rhode Island, active
1830-1845
Mark refs.: A. CFM, p. 226. B-F.
LIL, vol. 2, p. 111; CFM, p. 226.
Marks:

A

B

C

D

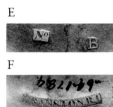

E

F

George Richardson
75. Teapot
Marks: B-F, outside bottom.
H. 11⅜ in.
64.1785

75

76

George Richardson
76. Teapot
Marks: B-F, outside bottom.
H. 9⅝ in.
64.1784

George Richardson
78. Sugar bowl
Marks: B-F, outside bottom.
H. 5⅛ in.
64.1802

George Richardson
79. Slop basin
Mark: A, on rim top. H. 4½ in.,
D. of rim 11⅝ in.
64.1866

78

79

John Skinner

1733-1813

Boston, Massachusetts, active
1760-1790

Mark refs.: A. LIL, vol. 1, 293;
CFM, p. 227. B. LIL, vol. 1, 294.

Marks:

A

B

John Skinner

87. Plate

Marks: A, B. H. ½ in., D. of rim
7¾ in., W. of rim 1 in.
64.2303

87

Eben Smith

Beverly, Massachusetts, active
ca. 1814-1856
Mark refs.: A. LIL, vol. 2, p. 113;
CFM, p. 227.
Mark:
A

Eben Smith
92. Teapot
Mark: A, inside bottom. H. 8½ in.
64.1789

92

94

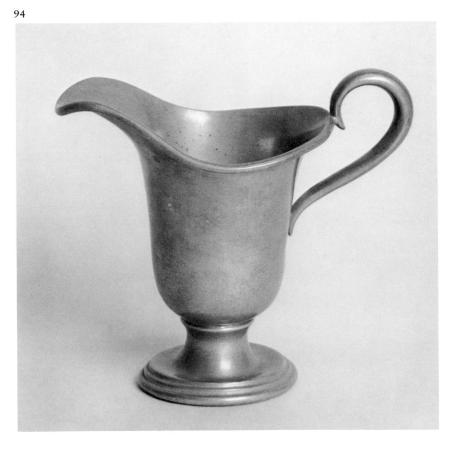

L. B. Smith

Boston, Massachusetts
Mark refs.: A. None.
Mark:
A

L. B. Smith
94. Cream pitcher
Mark: A, outside bottom. H. 4⅞ in.
64.1803

Smith & Company

Boston, Massachusetts, active
1847-1849
Mark ref.: LIL, vol. 2, p. 113.
Mark:
A

Smith & Company
95. Lamp
Mark: A, outside bottom. H. 5⅝ in.
64.1835

Smith & Company
96. Teapot
Mark: A, outside bottom.
H. 10¾ in.
64.1788

95

96

Taunton Britannia Manufacturing Company

Taunton, Massachusetts, active
1830-1834
Mark refs.: A. LIL, vol. 2, p. 114;
CFM, p. 227.
Mark:
A

Taunton Britannia Manufacturing Company
97. Whale oil burner
Mark: A, outside bottom. H. 6⅝ in.
64.1836

97

Israel Trask

1786-1867

Beverly, Massachusetts, active
ca. 1813-ca. 1856
Mark refs.: A. LIL, vol. 2, p. 114;
CFM, p. 227.
Mark:
A

Israel Trask

98. Footed baptismal bowl
Mark: A, outside bottom. H. 4⅛
in., D. of rim 10¾ in., D. of base,
4¾ in., W. of rim 1⅝ in.
64.1857

Israel Trask

100. Cruet set
Mark: A, outside bottom. H. 8½ in.
64.1862, a-f

98

Oliver Trask

1792-1847

Beverly, Massachusetts, active
1832-1839

Mark refs.: A. LIL, vol. 2, p. 115;
CFM, p. 227.

Mark:

A

Oliver Trask

103. Footed baptismal bowl
Mark: A, outside bottom. H. 5¼
in., D. of rim 10⅝ in., D. of base
5½ in., W. of rim 1⅝ in.
64.1856

Oliver Trask

106. Beaker
Mark: A, outside bottom. H. 5⅛
in., D. of rim 3⅜ in., D. of base
2⅝ in.
Purchased of F. H. Bigelow. 14.935

Oliver Trask

105. Flagon with spout
Mark: A, outside bottom. H. 10 in.,
D. of rim 4¼ in., D. of base 6 in.
Purchased of F. H. Bigelow.
14.929

103

106

105

Oliver Trask
104. Flagon with spout
Mark: A, outside bottom. H. 11 in.,
D. of rim 5⅛ in., D. of base 5½ in.
64.1735

104

J. B. Woodbury

Probably Beverly, Massachusetts,
active ca. 1830-1835;
Philadelphia, Pennsylvania,
active 1835-1838
Mark refs.: A. LIL, vol. 2, p. 118;
CFM, p. 229. B. LIL, vol. 2, p. 118.
Marks:

A

B

J. B. Woodbury
107. Teapot
Mark: A, outside bottom. H. 4⅝ in.
Gift of J. T. Coolidge. 17.1602

107

J. B. Woodbury
108. Teapot
Mark: B, outside bottom.
H. 10¼ in.
64.1799

Connecticut

Luther Boardman

1812-1887
Chester and East Haddam,
Connecticut, active 1839-1870
Mark ref.: A, B. LIL, vol. 2, p. 97.
Marks:

A

B

Luther Boardman
110. Teapot
Mark: A, outside bottom. H. 7¼ in.
64.1768

Luther Boardman
111. Tablespoon
Mark: B, underside of handle.
L. 7⅞ in.
64.1882

110

111

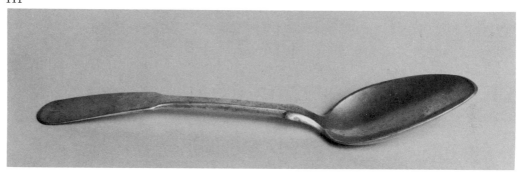

Thomas Danforth Boardman

1784 - 1873
Hartford, Connecticut, active
1804 - 1860 and later
Mark refs.: A. LIL, vol. 1, 424.
B. LIL, vol. 1, 427; CFM, p. 216.
Marks:

A

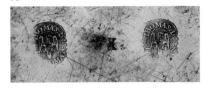

B

Thomas D. Boardman
114. Deep dish
Mark: A, twice. H. 1½ in., D. of
rim 11½ in., W. of rim 1⅛ in.
64.2307

Thomas D. Boardman
117. Basin
Mark: B, inside bottom. H. 1⅞ in.,
D. of rim 8 in., W. of rim ⅜ in.
64.2325

114
117

32

Thomas D. Boardman
116. Quart pot
Mark: B, outside bottom. H. 5⅞
in., D. of rim 4 in., D. of base 4¾ in.
64.2347

Thomas D. Boardman
115. Teapot
Mark: B, outside bottom. H. 8¾ in.
64.1794

116
115

Thomas D. Boardman
1784-1873
&
Sherman Boardman
1787-1861

Hartford, Connecticut, active
1810-1850

Mark refs.: A. LIL, vol. 1, 428;
CFM, p. 216. B. LIL, vol. 1, 433;
CFM, p. 217. C. LIL, vol 1, 435;
CFM, p. 217.

Marks:

A

B

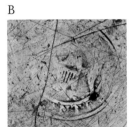

C

**Thomas D. Boardman &
Sherman Boardman**
123. Porringer
Mark: A, handle top. H. 2 in.,
D. of rim 5⅛ in.
64.2354

123

Thomas D. Boardman &
Sherman Boardman
122. Porringer
Mark: A, handle top. H. 1¼ in.,
D. of rim 4 in.
64.2353

Thomas D. Boardman &
Sherman Boardman
124. Porringer
Mark: A, on handle top. H. 1¾ in.,
D. of rim 5 in.
64.2352

122

124

Thomas D. Boardman &
Sherman Boardman
125. Beaker
Mark: A, outside bottom. H. 5⅛
in., D. of rim 3½ in., D. of base
2⅞ in.
64.1709

Thomas D. Boardman &
Sherman Boardman
126. Porringer
Mark: A, on handle top. H. 1¼ in.,
D. of rim 3⅞ in.
64.1745

125
126

Thomas D. Boardman &
Sherman Boardman
127. Teapot
Mark: A, outside bottom. H. 5⅝ in.
64.1796

Thomas D. Boardman &
Sherman Boardman
128. Basin
Mark: A, inside bottom. H. 1⅞ in.,
D. of rim 6½ in., W. of rim ¼ in.
64.2328

127

128

I. Curtis

Connecticut (?), active 1818-1825

or

Boardman & Company

New York City

or

Boardman & Hall

Philadelphia, Pennsylvania

Mark refs.: A. LIL, vol. 1, 452;
CFM, p. 217.

Mark:

A

I. Curtis (?)
134. Basin
Mark: A, inside bottom. H. 1⅝ in.,
D. of 6⅜ in., W. of rim ¼ in.
64.1694

134

John Danforth

1741 - ca. 1799

Norwich, Connecticut, active
1773 - 1793

Mark refs.: A. LIL, vol. 1, 357.
B. LIL, vol. 1, 353. C. LIL, vol. 1,
352; CFM, p. 219.

Marks:

A (attributed)

B

C

John Danforth

137. Porringer

Mark: A, handle top. H. 1⅝ in.,
D. of rim 4½ in.

64.1749

Joseph Danforth, Sr.

1758 - 1788

Middletown, Connecticut,
active 1780 - 1788

Mark refs.: A. LIL, vol. 1, 377;
CFM, p. 219. B. LIL, vol. 1, 378;
CFM, p. 219. C. LIL, vol. 1, 374;
CFM, p. 219.

Marks:

A

B

C

Joseph Danforth, Sr.

139. Mug

Mark: C, to left of handle joint.
H. 4⅜ in., D. of rim 3¼ in., D. of
base 3⅛ in.

Gift of Frances Hill Bigelow. 15.318

137
139

Josiah Danforth

1803-1872

Middletown, Connecticut,
active 1821-ca. 1843
Mark refs.: A. LIL, vol. 1, 395;
CFM, p. 219.
Mark:
A

Josiah Danforth
148. Teapot
Mark: A, outside bottom. H. 7⅝ in.
64.1771

Samuel Danforth

1774-1816

Hartford, Connecticut, active
1795-1816
Mark refs.: A. LIL, vol. 1, 403;
CFM, p. 220. B. LIL, vol. 1, 404;
CFM, p. 220. C. LIL, vol 1, 400;
CFM, p. 220. D. LIL, vol. 1, 398;
CFM, p. 220. E. LIL, vol. 1, 402;
CFM, p. 220. F. LIL, vol. 1, 401.
Marks:
A

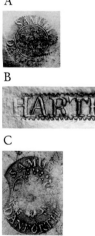

B

C

D

E

F Illegible, not illustrated

148

150

Samuel Danforth
150. Half pint mug
Mark: F, inside bottom. H. 3 in., D.
of rim 2⅝ in., D. of base 3 in.
64.1724

Samuel Danforth
151. Basin
Mark: A, inside bottom. H. 2 in.,
D. of rim 8⅛ in., W. of rim ⅜ in.
64.1698

Samuel Danforth
153. Beaker
Mark: E, outside bottom. H. 5¼
in., D. of rim 3½ in., D. of base 3 in.
64.1713

Samuel Danforth
154. Flagon
Marks: A, B, outside bottom.
H. 11½ in., D. of rim 4 in., D. of
base 6½ in.
64.1733

151

153

154

41

Thomas Danforth I

1703-1786

Taunton, Massachusetts, active 1727-1733; Norwich, Connecticut, 1733-ca. 1775

or

Thomas Danforth II

1731-1782

Middletown, Connecticut, active 1755-1782

or

Thomas Danforth III

or

Partnership between the three
Mark refs.: A. LIL, vol. 1, 362a;
CFM, p. 220. B. LIL, vol. 1, 364;
CFM, p. 220. C. LIL, vol 1, 365;
CFM, p. 220. D. LIL, vol. 1, 363a;
CFM, p. 220.
Marks:
A

B

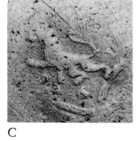

C

D

**Thomas Danforth I, II, or III,
or partnership**
162. Plate
Marks: B, D. H. ⅝ in., D. of rim
7⅞ in., W. of rim 1 in.
64.1641

162

42

Thomas Danforth III

1756-1840

Stepney, Connecticut, active
1777-1818; Philadelphia,
Pennsylvania, active 1807-1813
Mark refs.: A. LIL, vol. 1, 372;
CFM, p. 220. B. LIL, vol. 1, 371;
CFM, p. 220. C. LIL, vol. 1, 373;
CFM, p. 220. D. LIL, vol. 1, 369;
CFM, p. 220. E. LIL, vol. 1, 368;
CFM, p. 220.
Marks:

A

B

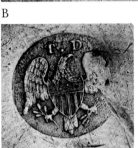

C

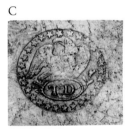

D

E Not illustrated

Thomas Danforth III
169. Basin
Mark: C, inside bottom. H. 1⅞ in.,
D. of rim 7⅞ in., W. of rim ⅜ in.
64.1701

Thomas Danforth III
174. Quart pot
Mark: E, inside bottom. H. 5⅞ in.,
D. of rim 4 in., D. of base 4⅝ in.
64.1725

169

174

Fuller & Smith

New London County,
Connecticut, active 1849-1851
Mark ref.: A. LIL, vol. 2, p. 102.
Mark:

A

Fuller & Smith

179. Pair of candlesticks with
inserts
Mark: A, outside bottom. H. 8¾ in.
64.1821a,b; 64.1822a,b

179

Ashbil Griswold

1784-1853

Meriden, Connecticut, active
1807-1835
Mark refs.: A. LIL, vol. 1, 421;
CFM, p. 222. B. LIL, vol. 1, 420.
C. LIL, vol. 1, 418.
Marks:

A

B

C

Ashbil Griswold
180. Beaker
Mark: A, outside bottom. H. 3 in.,
D. of rim 2⅞ in., D. of base 2¼ in.
64.1714

Ashbil Griswold
181. Shaving box
Mark: A, outside bottom. H. 1¾
in., D. of rim 5⅜ in., D. of base
3⅝ in.
64.1870

180
181

Ashbil Griswold
182. Teapot
Mark: B, outside bottom.
H. 10¼ in.
64.1775

182

Isaac C. Lewis
b. 1812
Meriden, Connecticut, active
1834-1852
Mark ref.: LIL, vol. 2, 106.
Mark:

A

Isaac C. Lewis
190. Teapot
Mark: A, outside bottom.
H. 10⅜ in.
64.1776

190

William W. Lyman

b. 1821

Meriden, Connecticut, active
1844-1852

Mark ref.: A. LIL, vol. 2, p. 107.

Mark:

A

William W. Lyman

191. Teapot

Mark: A, outside bottom.

H. 10⅜ in.

64.1777

191

Thomas Mix

Meriden, Connecticut, active
ca. 1826

Mark ref.: A. LIL, vol. 3, p. 186.

Mark:

A

Thomas Mix

192. Tablespoon

Mark: A, underside of handle top.

L. 7⅞ in.

64.1883

192

Hiram Yale
1799-1831

H. Yale & Company
Wallingford, Connecticut,
active 1822-1831
Mark refs.: A. LIL, vol. 1, 444;
CFM, p. 229. B. LIL, vol. 1, 445.
Marks:
A

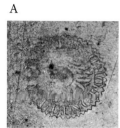

B

Hiram Yale
196. Teapot
Mark: A, inside bottom. H. 8⅛ in.
64.1800

196

Hiram Yale
197. Flagon with spout
Mark: B, outside bottom.
H. 10⅝ in., D. of rim 5½ in., D. of
base 5⅜ in.
Purchased of F. H. Bigelow. 14.926

197

William Yale
1784-1833
&
Samuel Yale
1787-1864

Meriden, Connecticut, active
1813-1820
Mark refs.: A. LIL, vol. 1, 440;
CFM, p. 229.
Mark:
A

William & Samuel Yale
198. Basin
Mark: A, inside bottom. H. 1¾ in.,
D. of rim 6⅝ in., W. of rim ¼ in.
64.1707

198

51

Rhode Island

Joseph Belcher
1729-1781
Joseph Belcher, Jr.
b. 1751/2

Newport, Rhode Island, active
1769-1784
Mark refs.: A. LIL, vol. 1, 314;
CFM, p. 216.
Mark:

A

Joseph Belcher
199. Dish
Mark: A, twice. H. ⅞ in., D. of
rim 11¼ in., W. of rim 1⅛ in.
64.1678

William Billings
1768-1813

Providence, Rhode Island, active
1791-1806
Mark refs.: A. LIL, vol. 1, 346;
CFM, p. 216. B. LIL, vol. 1, 347;
CFM, p. 216.
Marks:

A

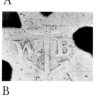

B

William Billings
200. Porringer
Mark: A, on handle top. H. 1½ in.
D. of rim 4⅞ in.
64.1746

199
200

52

William Calder

1792-1856

Providence, Rhode Island, active
1817-1856

Mark refs.: A. LIL, vol. 1, 350;
CFM, p. 218. B. LIL, vol. 1, 351;
CFM, p. 218. C. CFM, p. 218.

Marks:

A

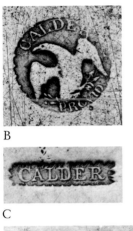

B

C

207
206

William Calder
207. Beaker
Mark: B, inside bottom. H. 3 in.,
D. of rim 3 in., D. of base 2¼ in.
64.1712

William Calder
206. Porringer
Mark: A, on handle top. H. 1⅜ in.,
D. of rim 4⅞ in.
64.1747

205

Samuel Hamlin

1746-1801

Hartford, Connecticut, active
1767-ca. 1768; Middletown,
Connecticut, active 1768-1773;
Providence, Rhode Island, active
1773-1801

Mark refs.: A. LIL, vol. 1, 330;
CFM, p. 222. B. LIL, vol. 1, 331;
CFM, p. 222. C. LIL, vol. 1, 336;
CFM, p. 222.

Marks:

A

B

C

Samuel Hamlin

218. Porringer
Mark: C, on handle top. H. 1⅞ in.,
D. of rim 5¼ in.
64.1755

Samuel Hamlin

215. Basin
Mark: A, inside bottom. H. 2 in.,
D. of rim 7⅝ in., W. of rim ⅜ in.
64.1703

218
215

Samuel Hamlin
217. Pint mug
Mark: A, to left of top handle
joint. H. 4¼ in., D. of rim 3¼ in.,
D. of base 3⅞ in.
64.1726

Samuel Hamlin
216. Quart pot
Marks: A, B, to left of top handle
joint. H. 5¾ in., D. of rim 4 in.,
D. of base 4⅜ in.
64.2348

217

216

56

Samuel E. Hamlin

1774-1864

Providence, Rhode Island, active
1801-1856
Mark ref.: A. LIL, vol. 1, 337.
Mark:
A

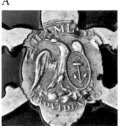

Samuel E. Hamlin
221. Porringer
Mark: A, handle top. H. 1⅞ in.,
D. of rim 5¼ in.
64.1753

221

Gershom Jones

1751-1809

Providence, Rhode Island, active
1774-1809

Mark refs.: A. LIL, vol. 1, 341.
B. LIL, vol. 1, 339; CFM, p. 223.
C. LIL, vol. 1, 342. D. LIL, vol. 1,
343. E. LIL, vol. 1, 344.

Marks:

A

B

C

D

E

Gershom Jones
222. Porringer
Mark: A, on handle top. H. 1⅜ in.,
D. of rim 4¼ in.
64.2358

Gershom Jones
224. Porringer
Mark: A, on handle top. H. 1¾ in.,
D. of rim 5⅜ in.
64.1756

222

224

58

David Melville

1755-1793
Newport, Rhode Island, active
1776-1793
Mark refs.: A. LIL, vol. 1, 322;
CFM, p. 225. B. LIL, vol. 1, 324;
CFM, p. 225. C. LIL, vol. 1, 318a;
CFM, p. 225.
Marks:

A

B

C

228

229

David Melville
228. Porringer
Mark: B, on handle top. H. 1⅝ in.,
D. of rim 4⅝ in.
64.1760

David Melville
229. Porringer
Mark: A, handle top; "TM" (for
Thomas Melville?) cast in handle
bracket. H. 1½ in., D. of rim 5 in.
64.1759

Thomas Melville

d. 1796
Newport, Rhode Island, active
1793-1796
Mark ref.: A. LIL, vol. 1, 325.
Mark:
A

Thomas Melville
235. Porringer
Mark: A, on handle bracket.
H. ½ in., D. of rim 5 in.
64.1762

235
236

Josiah Miller

Rhode Island or Connecticut,
active ca. 1725-1775
Mark ref.: A. CFM, p. 203.
Mark:
A

Josiah Miller
236. Sundial
Mark: A, on face. D. 4½ in.
64.1859

60

W. Potter

Probably New England, active
ca. 1830-1840
Mark refs.: A. LIL, vol. 2, p. 110;
CFM, p. 226.
Mark:

A

W. Potter
237. Sander
Mark: A, outside bottom. H. 2¼
in., D. of rim 2⅛ in., D. of base
2⅛ in.
64.1868

237

New York

Francis Bassett I

1690-1758
New York City, active 1718-
1758
Mark refs.: A. LIL, vol. 2, 461;
CFM, p. 215. B. LIL, vol. 2, 460.
Marks:

A

B

Francis Bassett I
238. Plate
Marks: A, twice; B, once. H. ¾ in.,
D. of rim 9⅜ in., W. of rim 1⅛ in.
64.1617

238

Frederick Bassett

1740-1800

New York City, active 1761-
1780; Hartford, Connecticut,
active 1780-1785; New York
City, active 1785-1799
Mark refs.: A. LIL, vol. 2, 465;
CFM, p. 215. B. LIL, vol. 2, 464;
CFM, p. 215. C. LIL, vol. 2, 466;
CFM, p. 215. D. LIL, vol. 2, 467;
CFM, p. 215.
Marks:

A

B

C

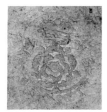

D

239

Frederick Bassett
239. Quart tankard
Mark: A, inside bottom. H. 5⅜ in.,
D. of rim ⅜ in., D. of base 5 in.
64.1739

Boardman & Company

New York City, active 1825-
1827
Mark refs.: A. LIL, vol. 1, 430.
B. LIL, vol. 1, 431; CFM, p. 217.
Marks:
A

B

Boardman & Company
247. Covered sugar bowl
Mark: B, outside bottom. H. 5¼ in.
64.1801

Boardman & Company
246. Flagon with spout
Mark: B, outside bottom. H. 8½
in., D. of rim 4⅛ in., D. of base 5 in.
64.1732

247

Timothy Boardman & Company

(Timothy Boardman, 1798-1825)
New York City, active 1822-1825
Mark refs.: A. LIL, vol. 1, 432; CFM, p. 217.
Mark:
A

Boardman & Hart

(T. D. & S. Boardman & Lucius Hart)
New York City, active 1828-1853
Mark refs.: A. None under Boardman & Hart. B. LIL, vol. 1, 437; CFM, p. 217. C. LIL, vol. 1, 439; CFM, p. 217. D. LIL, vol. 1, 436; CFM, p. 217.
Marks:
A

B

C

D

251

256

Timothy Boardman & Company
251. Beaker
Mark: A, outside bottom. H. 5⅛ in., D. of rim 3½ in., D. of base 2¾ in.
64.1710

Boardman & Hart
256. Beaker
Marks: B, C, outside bottom. H. 5⅛ in., D. of rim 3½ in., D. of base 2⅞ in.
64.1708

Boardman & Hart
255. Teapot
Marks: B, C, outside bottom. H. 8⅝ in.
64.1769

Boardman & Hart
257. Plate
Marks: A, twice; B, C, once. H. ⅞ in., D. 9⅜ in., W. of rim 1⅛ in.
Purchased of F. H. Bigelow. 14.930

255
257

Timothy Brigden

1774-1819

Albany, New York, active 1816-1819

Mark refs.: A. LIL, vol. 2, 519; CFM, p. 218.

Mark:

A

Timothy Brigden

263. Chalice

Mark: A, bottom of bowl and inside base. H. 9 in., D. of rim 4 in., D. of base 4½ in.

64.1742

263

Ephraim Capen & George Molineux

New York City, active 1848-1854

Mark refs.: A. LIL, vol. 2, p. 99;
CFM, p. 218.

Mark: A

A

Ephraim Capen & George Molineux
264. Nursing or sparking lamp
Mark: A, outside bottom. H. 2⅞ in.
64.1826

264

266

Daniel Curtiss

1799/1800-1872

Albany, New York, active 1822-1840

Mark refs.: A. LIL, vol. 2, 522;
CFM, p. 219. B. LIL, vol. 2, 523;
CFM, p. 219.

Marks:

A

B

Daniel Curtiss
266. Cuspidor
Mark: B, inside base. H. 3¼ in.,
D. of rim 5¾ in., D. of base 4½ in.
64.1874

Edmund Endicott
&
William F. Sumner

New York City, active 1746-
1851
Mark refs.: A. LIL, vol. 2, p. 101;
CFM, p. 221. B. LIL, vol. 2, p. 101.
Marks:
A

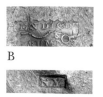

B

Edmund Endicott & William F.
Sumner
270. Lamp
Marks: A, B, outside bottom.
H. 3¾ in.
64.1829

270

271

Gaius Fenn
&
Jason Fenn

New York City, active 1831-
1843
Mark refs.: A. LIL, vol. 2, p. 101;
CFM, p. 222.
Mark:
A

Gaius & Jason Fenn
271. Inkwell
Marks: A, outside bottom.
H. 1¾ in., D. of rim 2½ in., D. of
base 2½ in.
64.1871

Henry Hopper

New York City, active 1842-1847

Mark refs.: A. LIL, vol. 2, p. 105; CFM, p. 223.

Mark:

A

Henry Hopper
273. Ladle
Mark: A, underside of handle top.
L. 13¼ in., D. of bowl 3⅞ in.
64.1878

Henry Hopper
272. Pair of candlesticks with inserts
Mark: A, outside bottom.
H. 10⅛ in.
64.1815a, b; 64.1816a, b

273
272

Charles Ostrander
&
George Norris

New York City, active 1848-1850

Mark refs.: A. LIL, vol. 2, p. 108; CFM, p. 225.

Mark:

A

Charles Ostrander & George Norris

275. Saucer candlestick with insert
Mark: A, outside bottom.
H. 5¼ in.
64.1820a, b

275

277

Renton & Company

New York City, active 1830's

Mark refs.: Carl Jacobs, *Guide to American Pewter* (New York, 1957), p. 150.

Mark:

A

Renton & Company

277. Lamp
Mark: A, outside bottom. H. 2⅛ in.
64.1832

Spencer Stafford
1772-1844

Albany, New York, active
ca. 1820-1827
Mark refs.: A. LIL, vol. 2, 512a.
B. LIL, vol. 2, 517; CFM, p. 227.
C. LIL, vol. 2, 520; CFM, p. 227.
Marks:

A

B

C

Spencer Stafford
278. Deep dish
Marks: B, C. H. 1⅜ in., D. of rim
13½ in., W. of rim 1⅝ in.
64.1688

278

James Weekes

New York City, active 1820-
1835
Mark refs.: A. LIL, vol. 2, p. 115;
CFM, p. 227.
Mark:
A

James Weekes
280. Beaker
Mark: A, outside bottom.
H. 3⅛ in., D. of rim 2⅞ in., D. of
base 2⅛ in.
64.1717

280

284

Thomas Wildes

New York City, active 1833-
1840
Mark refs.: A. LIL, vol. 2, p. 117;
CFM, p. 228.
Mark:
A

Thomas Wildes
284. Saucer lamp
Mark: A, outside bottom. H. 4⅛ in.
64.1838

Henry Will

ca. 1735 - ca. 1802

New York City, active 1761-
1755, 1783-1793; Albany, New
York, active 1776-1783

Mark refs.: A. LIL, vol. 2, 492.
B. LIL, vol. 2, 491; CFM, p. 228.

Marks:

A

B

Henry Will

286. Quart tankard
Mark: B, inside bottom. H. 6⅞ in.,
D. of rim 4⅜ in., D. of base 4⅞ in.
64.1741

Henry Will

285. Basin
Mark: A, inside bottom. H. 1⅞ in.,
D. of rim 8 in., W. of rim ⅜ in.
64.1706

286

285

Peter Young

1749-1813

New York City, active 1775-
1785; Albany, New York, active
1785-1795
Mark refs.: A. LIL, vol. 2, 515.
Mark:
A

Peter Young
288. Chalice
Mark: A, outside base. H. 8½ in.,
D. of rim 4 in., D. of base 4⅜ in.
64.1743

288

Pennsylvania

Blakeslee Barns
1781-1823
Philadelphia, Pennsylvania,
active 1812-1817
Mark refs.: A. LIL, vol. 2, 551;
CFM, p. 215. B. LIL, vol. 2, 553;
CFM, p. 215.
Marks:
A

B Not illustrated

Blakeslee Barns
289. Deep dish
Mark: A. H. 1⅜ in., D. of rim
11⅛ in., W. of rim 1¼ in.
64.1676

Parks Boyd
1771/2-1819
Philadelphia, Pennsylvania,
active 1795-1819
Mark refs.: A. LIL, vol. 2, 544;
CFM, p. 217. B. LIL, vol. 2, 546;
CFM, p. 217.
Marks:
A

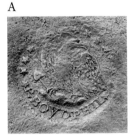

B

Parks Boyd
293. Pint mug
Mark: B, inside bottom. H. 4⅛ in.,
D. of rim 3¼ in., D. of base 3⅞ in.
64.1722

289

293

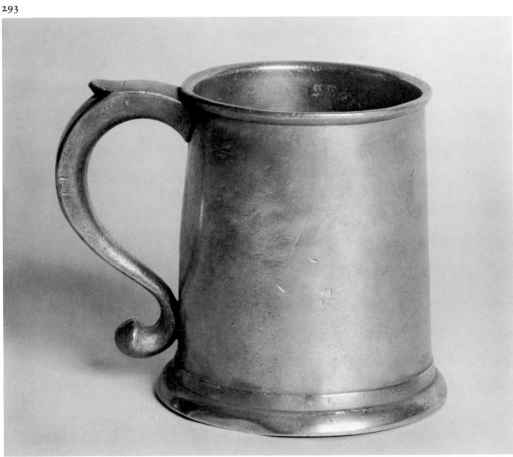

294

Parks Boyd
294. Teapot
Mark: B, inside bottom. H. 6 in.
64.1795

Louis Kruiger

Philadelphia, Pennsylvania,
active 1830's
Mark ref.: A. LIL, vol. 2, p. 106.
Mark:
A

Louis Kruiger
299. Ladle
Mark: A, underside of handle top.
L. 13½ in., D. of bowl 3⅜ in.
64.1888

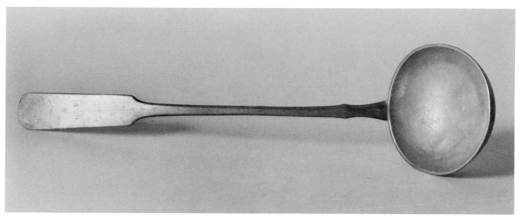

299

300

William McQuilkin

Philadelphia, Pennsylvania,
active 1839-1853
Mark refs.: A. LIL, vol. 2, p. 107;
CFM, p. 224.
Mark:
A

William McQuilkin
300. Water pitcher
Mark: A, outside bottom. H. 12 in.
64.1810

John H. Palethorp & Robert Palethorp, Jr.

1797-1822

Philadelphia, Pennsylvania, active separately and in partnership 1817-1845

Mark refs.: A. LIL, vol. 2, 559; CFM, p. 225. B. LIL, vol. 2, 561. C. LIL, vol. 2, p. 108; CFM, p. 225.

Marks:

A

B

C

Palethorps
301. Plate
Mark: B. H. ½ in., D. of rim 7¾ in., W. of rim 1⅛ in.
64.1659

Palethorps
302. Beaker
Mark: C, inside bottom. H. 3⅛ in., D. of rim 2⅞ in., D. of base 2 in.
64.1716

301
302

William Will

1742-1798

Philadelphia, Pennsylvania,
active 1764-1798
Mark refs.: A. LIL, vol. 2, 537;
CFM, p. 229. B. LIL, vol. 2, 540;
CFM, p. 229. C. LIL, vol. 2, 539;
CFM, p. 229. D. LIL, vol. 2, 541;
CFM, p. 229.
Marks:

A

B

C

D

William Will
306. Basin
Mark: D, inside bottom. H. 1⅜ in.,
D. of rim 6¼ in., W. of rim ¼ in.
64.1705

William Will
305. Quart pot
Mark: C, inside bottom. H. 5⅞ in.,
D. of rim 3⅞ in., D. of base 4¾ in.
64.1728

306

305

Lorenzo L. Williams

Philadelphia, Pennsylvania,
active 1838-1842
Mark ref.: A. LIL, vol. 2, p. 117.
Mark:
A

Lorenzo L. Williams
308. Baptismal bowl
Mark: A, outside bottom. H. 4⅝
in., D. of rim 6⅝ in., D. of base
4¼ in.
64.1858

308

Maryland

George Lightner
1749-1815
Baltimore, Maryland, active
1806-1815
Mark refs.: A. LIL, vol. 2, 566;
CFM, p. 224.
Mark: A
A

George Lightner
313. Plate
Mark: A, twice. H. ½ in., D. of rim
7¾ in., W. of rim 1 in.
64.1655

313

Unknown Makers

Unknown Maker, "I. C."
Probably Boston, Massachusetts
Mark refs.: A. LIL, vol. 2, 576;
CFM, p. 150.
Mark:
A

319. Porringer, crown handle
Mark: A, cast in handle bracket.
H. 1⅝ in., D. of rim 4⅝ in.
64.1751

Unknown Maker, "E. C."
New York or New England
Mark refs.: A. LIL, vol. 2, 572;
CFM, p. 151.
Mark:
A

320. Porringer, "old English"
handle
Mark: A, cast in handle bracket.
H. 1⅜ in., D. of rim 4½ in.
64.1750

319

320

Unknown Maker
Probably Newport, Rhode Island
321. Porringer, triangular handle
No mark. "M E" stamped on handle top, owner or maker? H. 1⅝
in., D. of rim 5 in.
64.1764

Unknown Maker
Probably Hartford, Connecticut
322. Porringer, dolphin handle
No mark. H. 1⅞ in., D. of rim
5¾ in.
64.1766

321

322

Unknown Maker
Probably New England, 1800-1830
323. Porringer, heart-shaped
handle
No mark. H. 1 in., D. of rim 3⅜ in.
64.1767

Unknown Maker
Probably Rhode Island or
Connecticut
324. Porringer, flower handle
No mark. H. 1½ in., D. of rim
4¼ in.
64.1765

323

324

Unknown Maker, "T. S."
Possibly American, probably
English
Mark ref.: A. LIL, vol. 2, 595.
Mark:
A

325. Quart tankard, domed lid,
tulip form body
Mark: A, inside bottom. H. 6 in.,
D. of rim 4⅛ in., D. of base 4½ in.
64.1740

325

Unknown Maker, "W. R."
Possibly American, probably
English
326. Quart tankard, domed lid,
tulip form body
Mark: "W R" under a crown to
left of top handle joint (not illustrated). H. 5⅞ in., D. of rim 4¼
in., D. of base 4¾ in.
Gift of Mr. and Mrs. William
deForest Thomson. 19.553

326

Unknown Maker
Probably Newport, Rhode Island,
or Boston, Massachusetts,
ca. 1750-1775
Mark refs.: A. LIL, vol. 2, 578,
vol. 3, 729.
Mark:
A

327. Quart pot
Mark: A, inside bottom. H. 5⅞ in.,
D. of rim 3⅞ in., D. of base 4¾ in.
Lent by Mrs. George A. Marks.
146.1972

327

Unknown Maker, "C. I."
Probably New England
328. Quart tankard, domed lid,
flared body
Mark: "C I" cast in handle. H. 6⅜
in., D. of rim 4⅛ in., D. of base
4⅝ in.
64.1737

328

Unknown Maker
Probably New York
329. Quart tankard, flat lid
No mark. H. 5⅜ in., D. of rim 4¼
in., D. of base 4¾ in.
64.1738

329

Unknown Maker
330. Fireman's trumpet
No mark. L. 16¾ in., D. of horn
opening 7⅝ in.
64.1875

Unknown maker
331. Ladle
No mark. L. overall 14 in., D. of
bowl 3¾ in.
64.1889

Unknown maker
332. Egg tongs
No mark. "1809" stamped on
handle side. L. 8 in.
64.1892

Unknown maker
333. Cream pitcher
No mark. H. 5⅞ in.
64.1808

330

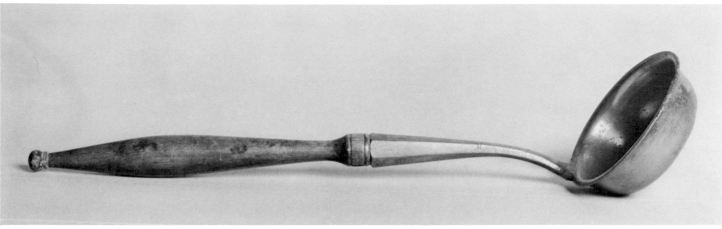

331

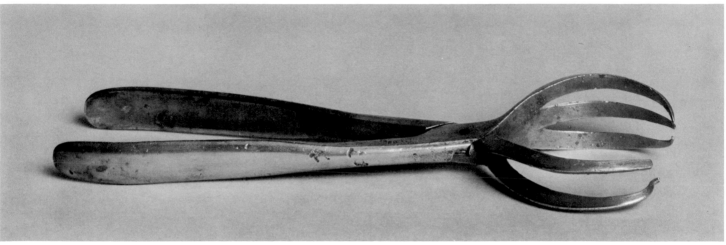

332

333

334

Unknown maker
334. Flagon with spout
No mark. H. 10⅞ in., D. of rim 3¾
in., D. of base 6½ in.
64.1736

Unknown maker
335. Lamp
No mark. H. 11 in.
64.1842

335

Unknown maker
336. Beaker
No mark. Engraved "Keziah
Kimball/and/Isaac Felch/May 3,
1826." H. 3 in., D. of rim 3 in., D.
of base 2¼ in.
64.2342

Unknown maker
337. Spoon mold
No mark. L. 7⅝ in. Refs.: LIL,
vol. 3, 750, 751.
64.1886

336

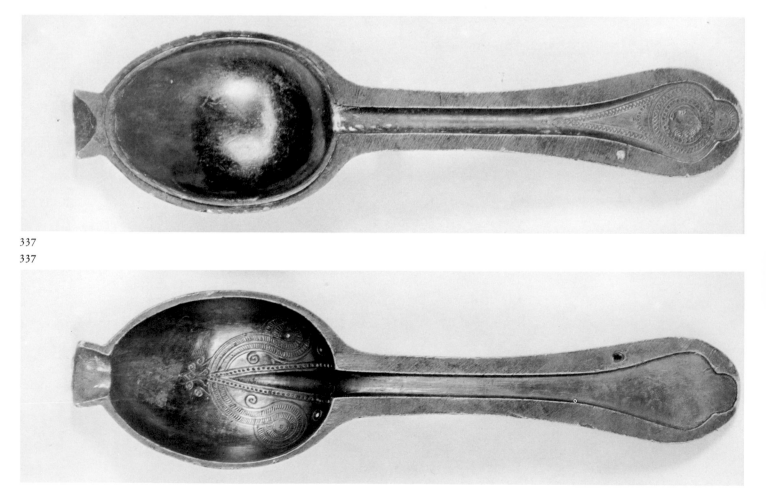

337

337

Unknown maker
338. Funnel
No mark. H. 4 in., D. 3½ in.
Gift of Mr. and Mrs. William
deForest Thomson. 19.555

Unknown maker
340. Salt
No mark. H. 2½ in., D. of rim
2⅝ in., D. of base 2⅞ in.
Bequest of Bessie Paine Bigelow.
24.174

338

340

339

Unknown maker
339. Teapot stand
No mark. L. 6⅛ in.
64.1869

341

Unknown maker
341. Teapot
No mark. H. 6¼ in.
64.1791

Unknown maker
342. Bullseye lamp
No mark. "Patent" stamped on
lense holder top. H. 8½ in.
64.1840

342

Checklist

of American Pewter
in the Museum of Fine Arts
Boston

Unless otherwise indicated,
pieces are from the bequest of
Mrs. Stephen S. FitzGerald.

Dimensions are to the nearest
⅛ inch.

An asterisk signifies that the
object is illustrated.

Maine

Rufus Dunham
1815 - ca. 1882
Westbrook, Maine, active
1837 - 1860

1. Flagon with spout*
Mark: A, outside bottom. H. 8⅜
in., D. of rim, 5⅜ in., D. of base,
6⅝ in.
Gift of the Congregational Church,
Greenland, New Hampshire.
12.1525

2. Teapot
Mark: B, outside bottom.
H. 11¼ in.
64.1797

3. Teapot*
Mark: B, outside bottom. H. 8⅜ in.
64.1772

4. Water Pitcher*
Mark: A, outside bottom. H. 8½ in.
64.1806

Allen Porter
Westbrook, Maine, active
1830 - 1840

5. Lamp
Mark: A, outside bottom. H. 5⅞ in.
64.1830

6. Teapot*
Mark: A, outside bottom.
H. 10⅝ in.
64.1783

Freeman Porter
b. 1808
Westbrook, Maine, active
1835 - 1865

7. Teapot*
Mark: A, outside bottom.
H. 10¾ in.
64.1782

8. Teapot
Mark: A, outside bottom. H. 7¼ in.
64.1781

9. Teapot*
Mark: A, outside bottom. H. 6⅜ in.
64.1780

Vermont

Richard Lee, Sr.
1747 - 1823
Grafton, New Hampshire, active
1788 - 1790; Ashfield, Massachusetts, active 1791 - 1793;
Lanesborough, Massachusetts,
active 1794 - 1802; Springfield,
Vermont, active 1802 - 1820
or

Richard Lee, Jr.
b. 1775
Springfield, Vermont, active
1795 - 1816

10. Porringer*
Mark: A, handle top. H. 1⅛ in.,
D. of rim 3¾ in.
64.1758

Massachusetts

Nathaniel Austin
1741 - 1816
Charlestown, Massachusetts,
active 1763 - 1807

11. Quart pot*
Mark: A, on terminal. H. 5¾ in.,
D. of rim, 3⅞ in. D. of base, 4⅞ in.
Gift of Francis H. Bigelow. 17.171

12. Basin
Mark: B, inside bottom. H. 1⅞ in.,
D. of rim 7⅞ in., W. of rim ⅜ in.
64.2323

13. Dish
Marks: B, C. H. ¾ in., D. of rim
12⅛ in., W. of rim 1¾ in.
64.1672

14. Plate
Marks: C, D. H. ½ in., D. of rim
8¾ in., W. of rim 1 in.
64.1609

15. Plate
Marks: C, D. H. ½ in., D. of rim
8 in., W. of rim 1 in.
64.1610

16. Plate
Marks: C, D. H. ½ in., D. of rim
8¾ in., W. of rim 1 in.
64.2261

17. Plate
Marks: C, D. H. ½ in., D. of rim
8⅝ in., W. of rim 1 in.
64.2262

18. Plate
Marks: B, C. H. ½ in., D. of rim
8¾ in., W. of rim 1 in.
64.2263

19. Plate
Marks: B, C. H. ½ in., D. of rim
8⅝ in., W. of rim 1 in.
64.2264

Richard Austin
1764 - 1817
Boston, Massachusetts, active
1793 - 1807

20. Basin*
Mark: B, inside bottom. H. 1⅞ in.,
D. of rim 8 in., W. of rim ⅜ in.
64.1691

21. Basin
Mark: B, inside bottom. H. 2 in.,
D. of rim 8 in., W. of rim ⅜ in.
64.2322

22. Dish
Marks: A, B. H. ¾ in., D. of rim
12⅛ in., W. of rim 1¾ in.
64.1673

23. Plate
Mark: A. H. ½ in., D. of rim 7¾
in., W. of rim ⅞ in.
64.1611

24. Plate
Mark: B. H. ½ in., D. of rim
8½ in., W. of rim 1 in.
64.1612

25. Plate
Mark: B. H. ½ in., D. of rim
8¾ in., W. of rim 1 in.
64.2265

26. Plate
Mark: B. H. ½ in., D. of rim
8⅞ in., W. of rim 1⅛ in.
64.2266

27. Plate
Mark: A. H. ½ in., D. of rim
7¾ in., W. of rim 1 in.
64.2267

28. Plate
Mark: A. H. ½ in., D. of rim
7⅞ in., W. of rim 1 in.
64.2268

Thomas Badger
1764-1826
Boston, Massachusetts, active
1787-1815

29. Basin*
Mark: A, inside bottom. H. 1⅞ in.,
D. of rim 8⅛ in., W. of rim ⅜ in.
64.2324

30. Plate
Marks: A, B. H. ½ in., D. of rim
7¾ in., W. of rim 1 in.
64.1613

31. Plate
Marks: B, C. H. ⅝ in., D. of rim
8⅜ in., W. of rim ⅞ in.
64.1614

32. Dish
Marks: A, B. H. ¾ in., D. of rim
12⅛ in., W. of rim 1⅜ in.
64.1674

33. Plate
Marks: A, B. H. ½ in., D. of rim
8½ in., W. of rim 1 in.
64.2269

34. Plate
Marks: A, B. H. ½ in., D. of rim
8½ in., W. of rim 1 in.
64.2271

35. Plate
Marks: A, B. H. ⅝ in., D. of rim
8⅜ in., W. of rim 1 in.
64.2273

36. Plate
Marks: A, B. H. ½ in., D. of rim
8⅞ in., W. of rim 1 in.
64.2274

37. Plate
Marks: A, B. H. ⅞ in., D. of rim
13½ in., W. of rim 1¾ in.
64.1675

38. Plate
Marks: A, B. H. ½ in., D. of rim
7¾ in., W. of rim 1 in.
64.2270

39. Plate
Marks: A, B. H. ⅝ in., D. of rim
8⅜ in., W. of rim 1⅛ in.
64.2272

Roswell Gleason
1799-1887
Dorchester, Massachusetts,
active 1821-1871

40. Coffee urn and drip pan*
Mark: Coffee urn, B, outside
bottom. H. 13⅝ in.
Mark: Drip pan, A, outside bottom.
H. 2⅜ in., D. of rim 6 in.
64.1867, 64.1873

41. Handled beaker, silvered*
Mark: A, outside bottom.
H. 4⅜ in., D. of rim 3⅜ in., D. of
base 3⅜ in.
64.2349

42. Pair of candlesticks*
Mark: A, outside bottom. H. 4¾ in.
64.1813 a,b; 64.1814 a,b

43. Candlestick (one of a pair)*
Mark: A, outside bottom. H. 7 in.
64.1812

44. Pair of candlesticks
Mark: A, outside bottom. H. 6⅝ in.
Purchased of F. H. Bigelow.
14.936, 937

45. Teapot*
Mark: A, outside bottom. H. 7¾ in.
64.1773

46. Miniature tea set*
Attributed to Roswell Gleason
Mark: none. Teapot: H. 3⅛ in.;
sugar bowl: H. 2 in.; slop basin:
H. 1⅞ in.; cream pitcher: H. 2⅜
in.; teacup with saucer: H. ⅞ in.
Given anonymously. Res. 28.71

47. Bedpan*
Mark: B, outside bottom. D. of
rim 11 in.
64.1877

48. Water pitcher*
Mark: B, outside bottom. H. 12 in.
64.1807

49. Water pitcher
Mark: A, outside bottom. H. 6⅞ in.
Gift of Miss Catherine Waters
Faucon. 28.277

50. Teapot*
Mark: A, outside bottom. H. 9⅞ in.
64.1774

51. Teapot
Mark: B, outside bottom.
H. 10½ in.
64.1798

52. Lamp
Mark: A, outside bottom. H. 4½ in.
64.1828

53. Lamp
Mark: A, outside bottom. H. 8⅛ in.
64.1855

54. Cruet set
Mark: A, outside bottom. H. 8⅜ in.
64.1860

55. Candlestick
Mark: A, outside bottom. H. 7 in.
64.1811

56. Syrup jug
Mark: A, outside bottom. H. 6¼ in.
64.2362

57. Plate
Mark: B. H. ⅞ in., D. of rim
9⅜ in., W. of rim 1⅛ in.
64.1644

58. Plate
Mark: B. H. ¾ in., D. of rim
9⅜ in., W. of rim 1⅛ in.
64.1645

59. Silvered baptismal bowl
Mark: B, outside bottom.

H. 5½ in., D. of rim 8⅛ in., D. of
base 5⅛ in.
Gift of the First Church of Newton.
1973.33

Samuel Green
ca. 1757 - ca. 1834
Boston, Massachusetts, active
ca. 1794 - 1834
60. Basin*
Mark: A, inside bottom. H. 1¾ in.,
D. of rim 7⅝ in., W. of rim ½ in.
Gift of Mrs. Edward M. Pickman.
63.1047

61. Plate
Mark: A. H. ½ in., D. of rim
8⅛ in., W. of rim 1 in.
64.1646

David B. Morey
&
R. H. Ober
Boston, Massachusetts, active
1852 - 1855
62. Handled beaker*
Mark: A, outside bottom. H. 3⅜
in., D. of rim 2⅛ in., D. of base
2¾ in.
64.1727

63. Teapot
Mark: A, outside bottom. H. 7¾ in.
64.1778

Samuel Pierce
1767 - 1840
Greenfield, Massachusetts,
active 1792 - 1830
Mark refs.: A. LIL, vol. 1, 406;
CFM, p. 226.
Mark:
A

64. Plate
Mark: A, twice. H. ⅝ in., D. of
rim 8 in., W. of rim 1⅛ in.
64.2294

65. Plate
Mark: A, twice. H. ⅝ in., D. of
rim 8 in., W. of rim 1⅛ in.
64.1660

66. Plate
Mark: A, twice. H. ⅝ in., D. of
rim 8 in., W. of rim 1⅛ in.
64.1661

67. Plate
Mark: A, twice. H. ⅝ in., D. of
rim 8 in., W. of rim 1⅛ in.
64.2295

68. Plate
Mark: A, twice. H. ⅝ in., D. of
rim 8 in., W. of rim 1⅛ in.
64.2296

69. Plate
Mark: A, twice. H. ⅝ in., D. of
rim 8 in., W. of rim 1 in.
64.2297

James H. Putnam
1803 - 1855
Malden, Massachusetts, active
1830 - 1855
70. Teapot*
Mark: A, outside bottom. H. 7⅞ in.
64.1787

71. Teapot*
Mark: A, outside bottom. H. 8 in.
64.2366

72. Syrup jug*
Mark: A, outside bottom. H. 4⅝ in.
64.1804

73. Lamp
Mark: A, outside bottom. H. 3¼ in.
64.1831

74. Plate
Mark: A. H. ¼ in., D. of rim
5¼ in., W. of rim ⅝ in.
64.1662

George Richardson
1782 - 1848
Boston, Massachusetts, active
1818 - 1828; Cranston, Rhode
Island, active 1830 - 1845
75. Teapot*
Marks: B - F, outside bottom.
H. 11⅜ in.
64.1785

76. Teapot*
Marks: B - F, outside bottom.

H. 9⅝ in.
64.1784

77. Teapot
Mark: A, outside bottom. H. 7¼ in.
64.1786

78. Sugar bowl*
Marks: B - F, outside bottom.
H. 5⅛ in.
64.1802

79. Slop basin*
Mark: A, on rim top. H. 4½ in.,
D. of rim 11⅝ in.
64.1866

Semper Eadem
(Perhaps Robert Bonynge)
Boston, Massachusetts, active
1725 - 1772
Mark refs.: A. LIL, vol. 1, 287a;
CFM, p. 227. B. LIL, vol. 1, 290;
CFM, p. 227. C. LIL, vol. 1, 292;
CFM, p. 217.

Marks:
A

B

C

80. Plate
Marks: A, B. H. ½ in., D. of rim
7¾ in., W. of rim 1 in.
64.1663

81. Plate
Mark: A. H. ⅝ in., D. of rim
8⅜ in., W. of rim 1 in.
64.2298

82. Plate
Mark: A. H. ½ in., D. of rim
8 in., W. of rim 1 in.
64.1664

83. Plate
Marks: A, B. H. ½ in., D. of rim

7⅝ in., W. of rim 1 in.
64.2299

84. Plate
Marks: A, B. H. ½ in., D. of rim
7⅝ in., W. of rim 1 in.
64.2301

85. Dish
Marks: A, B. H. ⅝ in., D. of rim
12⅛ in., W. of rim 1⅜ in.
64.2321

86. Plate
Marks: C, twice, A, once. H. ½ in.,
D. of rim 8¾ in., W. of rim 1 in.
64.1621

John Skinner
1733-1813
Boston, Massachusetts, active
1760-1790

87. Plate*
Marks: A, B. H. ½ in., D. of rim
7¾ in., W. of rim 1 in.
64.2303

88. Plate
Marks: A, B. H. ½ in., D. of rim
7¾ in., W. of rim 1 in.
64.2302

89. Plate
Marks: A, B. H. ⅝ in., D. of rim
8⅞ in., W. of rim 1⅛ in.
64.1666

90. Plate
Marks: A, B. H. ½ in., D. of rim
9 in., W. of rim 1⅛ in.
64.1667

91. Plate
Marks: A, B. H. ½ in., D. of rim
9 in., W. of rim 1⅛ in.
64.1668

Eben Smith
Beverly, Massachusetts, active
ca. 1814-1856

92. Teapot*
Mark: A, inside bottom. H. 8½ in.
64.1789

93. Lamp
Mark: A, outside bottom. H. 6⅛ in.
64.1833

L. B. Smith
Boston, Massachusetts

94. Cream pitcher*

Mark: A, outside bottom. H. 4⅞ in.
64.1803

Smith & Company
Boston, Massachusetts, active
1847-1849

95. Lamp*
Mark: A, outside bottom. H. 5⅝ in.
64.1835

96. Teapot*
Mark: A, outside bottom.
H. 10¾ in.
64.1788

Taunton Britannia Manufacturing Company
Taunton, Massachusetts, active
1830-1834

97. Whale oil burner*
Mark: A, outside bottom. H. 6⅝ in.
64.1836

Israel Trask
1786-1867
Beverly, Massachusetts, active
ca. 1813-ca. 1856

98. Footed baptismal bowl*
Mark: A, outside bottom. H. 4⅛
in., D. of rim 10¾ in., D. of base
4¾ in., W. of rim 1⅝ in.
64.1857

99. Flagon with spout
Mark: A, outside bottom.
H. 10¾ in., D. of rim 4 in., D. of
base 6 in.
64.1734

100. Cruet set*
Mark: A, outside bottom. H. 8½ in.
64.1862 a-f

101. Cruet set
Mark: A, outside bottom. H. 9 in.
64.1861 a-f

102. Lamp
Mark: A, outside bottom. H. 6⅛ in.
64.1837

Oliver Trask
1792-1847
Beverly, Massachusetts, active
1832-1839

103. Footed baptismal bowl*

Mark: A, outside bottom. H. 5¼
in., D. of rim 10⅝ in., D. of base
5½ in., W. of rim 1⅝ in.
64.1856

104. Flagon with spout*
Mark: A, outside bottom. H. 11 in.,
D. of rim 5⅛ in., D. of base 5½ in.
64.1735

105. Flagon with spout*
Mark: A, outside bottom. H. 10 in.,
D. of rim 4¼ in., D. of base 6 in.
Purchased of F. H. Bigelow. 14.929

106. Beaker*
Mark: A, outside bottom. H. 5⅛
in., D. of rim 3⅜ in., D. of base
2⅝ in.
Purchased of F. H. Bigelow. 14.935

J. B. Woodbury
Probably Beverly, Massachusetts,
active ca. 1830-1835; Philadelphia, Pennsylvania, active
1835-1838

107. Teapot*
Mark: A, outside bottom. H. 4⅝ in.
Gift of J. T. Coolidge. 17.1602

108. Teapot*
Mark: B, outside bottom.
H. 10¼ in.
64.1799

Connecticut

Stephen Barns
Probably Middletown or Wallingford, Connecticut, active 1791-1800
Mark refs.: A. LIL, vol. 1, 417; CFM, p. 215.
Mark: A, illegible, not illustrated.

109. Plate
Mark: A. H. ½ in., D. of rim 8 in., W. of rim 1 in.
64.1616

Luther Boardman
1812-1887
Chester and East Haddam, Connecticut, 1839-1870

110. Teapot*
Mark: A, outside bottom. H. 7¼ in.
64.1768

111. Tablespoon*
Mark: B, underside of handle. L. 7⅞ in.
64.1882

112. Tablespoon
Mark: B, underside of handle. L. 8 in.
64.1881

Thomas Danforth Boardman
1784-1873
Hartford, Connecticut, active 1804-1860 and later

113. Plate
Mark: A, twice. H. ⅝ in., D. of rim 7⅝ in., W. of rim 1 in.
64.1622

114. Deep dish*
Mark: A, twice. H. 1½ in., D. of rim 11½ in., W. of rim 1⅛ in.
64.2307

115. Teapot*
Mark: B, outside bottom. H. 8¾ in.
64.1794

116. Quart pot*
Mark: B, outside bottom. H. 5⅞ in., D. of rim 4 in., D. of base 4¾ in.
64.2347

117. Basin*
Mark: B, inside bottom. H. 1⅞ in.,
D. of rim 8 in., W. of rim ⅜ in.
64.2325

118. Deep dish
Mark: A, twice. H. 1⅜ in., D. of rim 11 in., W. of rim 1⅛ in.
64.2308

119. Plate
Mark: A, twice. H. ⅝ in., D. of rim 7⅝ in., W. of rim 1 in.
64.2278

120. Plate
Mark: B, twice. H. 1 in., D. of rim 9⅜ in., W. of rim 1¼ in.
Purchased of F. H. Bigelow. 14.931

Thomas D. Boardman
1784-1873

&

Sherman Boardman
1787-1861
Hartford, Connecticut, active 1810-1850

121. Basin
Mark: B, inside bottom. H. 2½ in., D. of rim 10⅛ in., W. of rim ½ in.
64.2327

122. Porringer*
Mark: A, handle top. H. 1¼ in., D. of rim 4 in.
64.2353

123. Porringer*
Mark: A, handle top. H. 2 in., D. of rim 5⅛ in.
64.2354

124. Porringer*
Mark: A, on handle top. H. 1¾ in., D. of rim 5 in.
64.2352

125. Beaker*
Mark: A, outside bottom. H. 5⅛ in., D. of rim 3½ in., D. of base 2⅞ in.
64.1709

126. Porringer*
Mark: A, on handle top. H. 1¼ in., D. of rim 3⅞ in.
64.1745

127. Teapot*
Mark: A, outside bottom. H. 5⅝ in.
64.1796

128. Basin*
Mark: A, inside bottom. H. 1⅞ in., D. of rim 6½ in., W. of rim ¼ in.
64.2328

129. Flagon with spout
Mark: A, outside bottom. H. 11 in., D. of rim 4 in., D. of base 5⅝ in.
64.1731

130. Plate
Mark: A. H. ½ in., D. of rim 6⅛ in., W. of rim ¾ in.
64.1624

131. Plate
Mark: C, twice. H. ¾ in., D. of rim 8½ in., W. of rim 1 in.
64.1626

132. Plate
Mark: B, twice. H. ⅞ in., D. of rim 9⅜ in., W. of rim 1¼ in.
Gift of the sons of the late Henry Forbes Bigelow. 43.92

133. Teapot
Mark: B, outside bottom. H. 7⅜ in.
64.2361

I. Curtis
Connecticut (?), active 1818-1825

or

Boardman & Company
New York City

or

Boardman & Hall
Philadelphia, Pennsylvania

134. Basin*
Mark: A, inside bottom. H. 1⅝ in., D. of rim 6⅜ in., W. of rim ¼ in.
64.1694

135. Bedpan
Mark: A, twice, outside bottom. D. of rim 10⅝ in.
64.1876

Edward Danforth
1765-1830
Middletown, Connecticut, active 1788-1790
Mark refs.: A, LIL, vol. 1, 387.
B. LIL, vol. 1, 388.
Marks:
A

136. Plate
Marks: A, twice, B, once. H. ¾ in.,
D. of rim 12⅛ in., W. of rim 1½ in.
64.1682

John Danforth
1741-ca. 1799
Norwich, Connecticut, active
1773-1793

137. Porringer*
Mark: A, handle top. H. 1⅝ in.,
D. of rim 4½ in.
64.1749

138. Plate
Marks: B, C. H. ⅝ in., D. of rim
7⅝ in., W. of rim 1 in.
64.1631

Joseph Danforth, Sr.
1758-1788
Middletown, Connecticut,
active 1780-1788

139. Mug*
Mark: C, to left of handle joint.
H. 4⅜ in., D. of rim 3¼ in., D. of
base 3⅛ in.
Gift of Francis Hill Bigelow. 15.318

140. Mug
Mark: C, to left of handle joint.
H. 4⅜ in., D. of rim 3¼ in., D. of
base 3¾ in.
64.1729

141. Dish
Marks: A, twice, B, once. H. 1⅝ in.,
D. of rim 13½ in., W. of rim 1⅜ in.
64.2312

142. Dish
Marks: A, twice, B, once. H. 1½ in.,
D. of rim 13 in., W. of rim 1⅜ in.
64.2313

143. Plate
Marks: A, twice, B, once. H. ⅝ in.,
D. of rim 8 in., W. of rim 1⅛ in.
64.1632

144. Plate
Marks: A, twice, B, once. H. ⅝ in.,
D. of rim 7⅞ in., W. of rim 1⅛ in.
64.1633

145. Plate
Marks: A, twice, B, once. H. ½ in.,
D. of rim 7⅞ in., W. of rim 1 in.
64.2285

146. Plate
Marks: A, twice, B, once. H. ⅝ in.,
D. of rim 7⅞ in., W. of rim 1⅛ in.
64.2286

147. Plate
Mark: A, twice. H. ⅝ in., D. of rim
7⅞ in., W. of rim 1⅛ in.
64.2287

Josiah Danforth
1803-1872
Middletown, Connecticut,
active 1821-ca. 1843

148. Teapot*
Mark: A, outside bottom. H. 7⅝ in.
64.1771

Samuel Danforth
1774-1816
Hartford, Connecticut, active
1795-1816

149. Beaker
Mark: F, outside bottom. H. 3 in.,
D. of rim 2¾ in., D. of base 2⅝ in.
64.2335

150. Half pint mug*
Mark: F, inside bottom. H. 3 in.,
D. of rim 2⅝ in., D. of base 3 in.
64.1724

151. Basin*
Mark: A, inside bottom. H. 2 in.,
D. of rim 8⅛ in., W. of rim ⅜ in.
64.1698

152. Plate
Mark: C. H.½ in., D. of rim 7⅞ in.,
W. of rim 1 in.
64.1635

153. Beaker*
Mark: E, outside bottom. H. 5¼
in., D. of rim 3½ in., D. of base
3 in.
64.1713

154. Flagon*
Marks: A, B, outside bottom.
H. 11½ in., D. of rim 4 in., D. of
base 6½ in.
64.1733

155. Basin
Mark: E, inside bottom. H. 1⅝ in.,

D. of rim 6⅝ in., W. of rim ¼ in.
64.1797

156. Quart pot
Marks: C, B, at base of handle joint.
H. 5⅝ in., D. of rim 4 in., D. of
base 4⅝ in.
64.1723

157. Plate
Mark: D, twice. H. ½ in., D. of rim
7⅞ in., W. of rim 1⅛ in.
64.1636

158. Dish
Marks: A, B. H. 1⅜ in., D. of rim
11½ in., W. of rim 1¼ in.
64.1683

159. Dish
Mark: C, twice. H. 1⅜ in., D. of
rim 11⅛ in., W. of rim 1¼ in.
64.2315

160. Plate
Mark: D, twice. H. ⅝ in., D. of rim
7⅞ in., W. of rim 1⅛ in.
64.1634

Thomas Danforth I
1703-1786
Taunton, Massachusetts, active
1727-1733; Norwich,
Connecticut, 1733-ca. 1775
or

Thomas Danforth II
1731-1782
Middletown, Connecticut,
active 1755-1782
or

Thomas Danforth III
or
Partnership between the three

161. Plate
Marks: A, twice, D, once. H. ½ in.,
D. of rim 7⅞ in., W. of rim 1 in.
64.1638

162. Plate*
Marks: B, D. H. ⅝ in., D. of rim
7⅞ in., W. of rim 1 in.
64.1641

163. Plate
Marks: A, D. H. ¾ in., D. of rim
9⅛ in., W. of rim 1⅛ in.
64.1639

164. Plate
Marks: A, twice, D, once. H. ½ in.,

D. of rim 7⅞ in., W. of rim 1 in.
64.1637

165. Dish
Marks: A, twice, D, once. H. 1⅝ in., D. of rim 13¼ in., W. of rim 1⅜ in.
64.2314

166. Plate
Marks: C, D. H. ⅝ in., D. of rim 7⅞ in., W. of rim 1 in.
64.1640

167. Plate
Marks: C, D. H. ⅝ in., D. of rim 7⅝ in., W. of rim 1 in.
64.2288

168. Dish
Marks: C, D. H. 1¼ in., D. of rim 11½ in., W. of rim 1¼ in.
64.2316

Thomas Danforth III
1756-1840
Stepney, Connecticut, active 1777-1818; Philadelphia, Pennsylvania, active 1807-1813

169. Basin*
Mark: C, inside bottom. H. 1⅞ in., D. of rim 7⅞ in., W. of rim ⅜ in.
64.1701

170. Plate
Marks: A, C. H. ⅝ in., D. of rim 7¾ in., W. of rim 1 in.
64.1642

171. Plate
Mark: B. H. 1⅜ in., D. of rim 11½ in., W. of rim 1¼ in.
64.2317

172. Deep dish
Marks: A, B. H. 1⅜ in., D. of rim 13⅛ in., W. of rim 1¾ in.
64.1684

173. Basin
Marks: D, E, inside bottom. H. 1 in., D. of rim 7⅞ in., W. of rim ¼ in.
64.1702

174. Quart pot*
Mark: E, inside bottom. H. 5⅞ in., D. of rim 4 in., D. of base 4⅝ in.
64.1725

William Danforth
Middletown, Connecticut, active 1792-1820

Mark ref.: A. LIL, vol. 1, 392.
Mark:
A

175. Deep dish
Mark: A, twice. H. 1⅜ in., D. of rim 13⅛ in., W. of rim 1¾ in.
64.1685

176. Plate
Mark: A, twice. H. ⅝ in., D. of rim 8 in., W. of rim 1⅛ in.
64.2289

177. Plate
Mark: A, twice. H. ⅝ in., D. of rim 8 in., W. of rim 1⅛ in.
64.2290

Thomas S. Derby
ca. 1786-1852
Middletown, Connecticut, active 1822-1850
Mark refs.: A. LIL, vol. 1, 441; CFM, p. 221.
Mark:
A

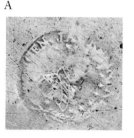

178. Basin
Mark: A, inside bottom. H. 1⅝ in., D. of rim 6½ in., W. of rim ⅜ in.
64.1695

Fuller & Smith
New London County, Connecticut, active 1849-1851

179. Pair of candlesticks with inserts*
Mark: A, outside bottom. H. 8¾ in.
64.1821a,b; 64.1822a,b

Ashbil Griswold
1784-1853
Meriden, Connecticut,

active 1807-1835

180. Beaker*
Mark: A, outside bottom. H. 3 in., D. of rim 2⅞ in., D. of base 2¼ in.
64.1714

181. Shaving box*
Mark: A, outside bottom. H. 1¾ in., D. of rim 5⅜ in., D of base 3⅝ in.
64.1870

182. Teapot*
Mark: B, outside bottom. H. 10¼ in.
64.1775

183. Beaker
Mark: A, outside bottom. H. 3 in., D. of rim 3 in., D. of base 2¼ in.
64.1715

184. Beaker
Mark: A, outside base. H. 2⅞ in., D. of rim 2¾ in., D. of base 2⅛ in.
64.2336

185. Dish
Mark: C, twice. H. 1 in., D. of rim 11 in., W. of rim 1 in.
64.1686

186. Dish
Mark: C, twice. H. 1½ in., D. of rim 13⅛ in., W. of rim 1⅜ in.
64.2365

187. Dish
Mark: C, twice. H. 1⅜ in., D. of rim 11⅛ in., W. of rim 1¼ in.
64.2318

Jehiel Johnson
1784/5-1833
Middletown, Connecticut, active 1815-1825; Fayetteville, North Carolina, active 1818-1819
Mark refs.: A. LIL, vol. 1, 447; CFM, p. 223.
Mark:
A

188. Plate
Mark: A, twice. H. ⅝ in., D. of rim 7⅞ in., W. of rim 1⅛ in.
64.1649

189. Plate
Mark: A, twice. H. ¾ in., D. of rim
8¾ in., W. of rim 1⅛ in.
64.1650

Isaac C. Lewis
b. 1812
Meriden, Connecticut, active
1834-1852
190. Teapot*
Mark: A, outside bottom.
H. 10⅜ in.
64.1776

William W. Lyman
b. 1821
Meriden, Connecticut, active
1844-1852
191. Teapot*
Mark: A, outside bottom.
H. 10⅜ in.
64.1777

Thomas Mix
Meriden, Connecticut, active
ca. 1826
192. Tablespoon*
Mark: A, underside of handle top.
L. 7⅞ in.
64.1883

193. Tablespoon
Mark: A, underside of handle top.
L. 7⅞ in.
64.1884

H. B. Ward & Company
Wallingford, Connecticut, active
ca. 1850
Mark ref.: A. LIL, vol. 2, p. 115.
Mark:
A

194. Teapot
Mark: A, outside bottom.
H. 11⅛ in.
64.1790

Jacob Whitmore
1736-1825
Middletown, Connecticut,
active 1758-1790

Mark refs.: A. LIL, vol. 1, 383;
CFM, p. 228.
Mark:
A

195. Plate
Mark: A, twice. H. ⅞ in., D. of rim
12¼ in., W. of rim 1½ in.
64.1690

Hiram Yale
1799-1831
H. Yale & Company
Wallingford, Connecticut,
active 1822-1831
196. Teapot*
Mark: A, inside bottom. H. 8⅛ in.
64.1800

197. Flagon with spout*
Mark: B, outside bottom. H. 10⅝
in., D. of rim 5½ in., D. of base
5⅜ in.
Purchased of F. H. Bigelow. 14.926

William Yale
1784-1833
&
Samuel Yale
1787-1864
Meriden, Connecticut, active
1813-1820
198. Basin*
Mark: A, inside bottom. H. 1¾ in.,
D. of rim 6⅝ in., W. of rim ¼ in.
64.1707

Rhode Island

Joseph Belcher
1729-1781
Joseph Belcher, Jr.
b. 1751/2
Newport, Rhode Island, active
1769-1784
199. Dish*
Mark: A, twice. H. ⅞ in., D. of rim
11¼ in., W. of rim 1⅛ in.
64.1678

William Billings
1768-1813
Providence, Rhode Island,
active 1791-1806
200. Porringer*
Mark: A, handle top. H. 1½ in.,
D. of rim 4⅞ in.
64.1746

201. Dish
Mark: B, three times. H. ⅞ in., D.
of rim 13¼ in., W. of rim 1¾ in.
64.1679

202. Plate
Mark: B, three times. H. ⅝ in., D.
of rim 8⅜ in., W. of rim 1 in.
64.1620

203. Plate
Mark: B, three times. H. ½ in., D.
of rim 7⅞ in., W. of rim 1 in.
64.2276

204. Plate
Mark: B, three times. H. ½ in., D.
of rim 7⅞ in., W. of rim 1 in.
64.2277

William Calder
1792-1856
Providence, Rhode Island, active
1817-1856
205. Teapot*
Mark: B, outside bottom.
H. 10¾ in.
64.1770

206. Porringer*
Mark: A, handle top. H. 1⅜ in.,
D. of rim 4⅞ in.
64.1747

207. Beaker*
Mark: B, inside bottom. H. 3 in.,

D. of rim 3 in., D. of base 2¼ in.
64.1712

208. Plate
Mark: A. H. ⅝ in., D. of rim 7⅞ in., W. of rim 1 in.
64.1630

209. Dish
Marks: B, C. H. 1⅛ in., D. of rim 11¾ in., W. of rim 1½ in.
64.1680

210. Dish
Mark: B. H. 1 in., D. 10¼ in., W. of rim 1¼ in.
64.2309

211. Dish
Mark: B. H. 1⅛ in., D. of rim 11⅜ in., W. of rim 1½ in.
64.2310

212. Plate
Mark: A. H. ⅝ in., D. of rim 8⅜ in., W. of rim 1 in.
64.2283

213. Plate
Mark: B. H. 1⅛ in., D. of rim 11⅜ in., W. of rim 1⅝ in.
Gift of the sons of the late Henry Forbes Bigelow. 43.93

214. Porringer
Mark: A, handle top. H. 1⅜ in., D. of rim 4⅞ in.
64.2355

Samuel Hamlin
1746-1801
Hartford, Connecticut, active 1767-ca. 1768; Middletown, Connecticut, active 1768-1773; Providence, Rhode Island, active 1773-1801

215. Basin*
Mark: A, inside bottom. H. 2 in., D. of rim 7⅝ in., W. of rim ⅜ in.
64.1703

216. Quart pot*
Marks: A, B, to left of top handle joint. H. 5¾ in., D. of rim 4 in., D. of base 4⅜ in.
64.2348

217. Pint mug*
Mark: A, to left of top handle joint. H. 4¼ in., D. of rim 3¼ in., D. of base 3⅞ in.
64.1726

218. Porringer*
Mark: C, handle top. H. 1⅞ in., D. of rim 5¼ in.
64.1755

219. Dish
Marks: A, B. H. 1¼ in., D. of rim 14⅞ in., W. of rim 1⅞ in.
64.1687

220. Plate
Marks: A, B. H. ½ in., D. of rim 9¼ in., W. of rim 1¼ in.
64.1647

Samuel E. Hamlin
1774-1864
Providence, Rhode Island, active 1801-1856

221. Porringer*
Mark: A, handle top. H. 1⅞ in., D. of rim 5¼ in.
64.1753

Gershom Jones
1751-1809
Providence, Rhode Island, active 1774-1809

222. Porringer*
Mark: A, handle top. H. 1⅜ in., D. of rim 4¼ in.
64.2358

223. Porringer
Mark: A, handle top. H. 1¾ in., D. of rim 5⅜ in.
64.2359

224. Porringer*
Mark: A, handle top. H. 1¾ in., D. of rim 5⅜ in.
64.1756

225. Plate
Marks: C, D, E. H. ⅝ in., D. of rim 8¼ in., W. of rim 1 in.
64.1652

226. Plate
Marks: B, twice, E, once. H. ⅝ in., D. of rim 8 in., W. of rim 1 in.
64.1653

227. Plate
Marks: B, twice, E, once. H. ½ in., D. of rim 8 in., W. of rim 1 in.
64.1654

David Melville
1755-1793
Newport, Rhode Island,

active 1776-1793

228. Porringer*
Mark: B, handle top. H. 1⅝ in., D. of rim 4⅝ in.
64.1760

229. Porringer*
Mark: A, handle top; "TM" (for Thomas Melville?) cast in handle bracket. H. 1½ in., D. of rim 5 in.
64.1759

230. Plate
Marks: A, twice, C. H. ½ in., D. of rim 8¼ in., W. of rim ⅞ in.
64.2293

231. Plate
Marks: A, twice, C. H. ½ in., D. of rim 8⅛ in., W. of rim ⅞ in.
64.1656

232. Plate
Marks: A, C. H. ½ in., D. of rim 8⅜ in., W. of rim 1 in.
64.1657

233. Dish
Marks: A, C. H. ¾ in., D. of rim 12⅛ in., W. of rim 1½ in.
64.2319

Samuel Melville
Newport, Rhode Island, active 1793-1796
Mark refs.: None
Mark:
A

234. Porringer
Mark: A, on handle bracket. H. 1¾ in., D. of rim 5¼ in.
64.1761

Thomas Melville
d. 1796
Newport, Rhode Island, active 1793-1796

235. Porringer*
Mark: A, on handle bracket. H. 1⅝ in., D. of rim 5 in.
64.1762

Josiah Miller
Rhode Island or Connecticut, active ca. 1725-1775

236. Sundial*
Mark: A, on face. D. 4½ in.
64.1859

W. Potter
Probably New England, active
ca. 1830-1840
237. Sander*
Mark: A, outside bottom. H. 2¼
in., D. of rim 2⅛ in., D. of base
2⅛ in.
64.1868

New York

Francis Bassett I
1690-1758
New York City, active 1718-
1758
238. Plate*
Marks: A, twice, B, once. H. ¾ in.,
D. of rim 9⅜ in., W. of rim 1⅛ in.
64.1617

Frederick Bassett
1740-1800
New York City, active 1761-
1780; Hartford, Connecticut,
active 1780-1785; New York
City, active 1785-1799
239. Quart tankard*
Mark: A, inside bottom. H. 5⅜ in.,
D. of rim ⅜ in., D. of base 5 in.
64.1739

240. Basin
Mark: A, inside bottom. H. 1½ in.,
D. of rim 6⅝ in., W. of rim ¼ in.
64.1692

241. Basin
Mark: A, outside bottom. H. 2 in.,
D. of rim 8 in., W. of rim ⅜ in.
64.1699

242. Plate
Marks: B, D. H. ⅝ in., D. of rim
8⅜ in., W. of rim 1 in.
64.1618

243. Dish
Marks: B, C, D. H. 1 in., D. of rim
13½ in., W. of rim 1¾ in.
64.2306

244. Plate
Marks: B, C. H. ½ in., D. of rim
8¾ in., W. of rim 1 in.
64.2275

245. Plate
Marks: B, C, D. H. ½ in., D. of rim
8⅜ in., W. of rim 1 in.
64.1619

Boardman & Company
New York City, active 1825-
1827
246. Flagon with spout*
Mark: B, outside bottom. H. 8½
in., D. of rim 4⅛ in., D. of base
5 in.
64.1732

247. Covered sugar bowl*
Mark: B, outside bottom. H. 5¼ in.
64.1801

248. Plate
Marks: A, twice, B, once. H. ⅞ in.,
D. of rim 9⅜ in., W. of rim 1¼ in.
64.1623

249. Plate
Mark: B, twice. H. ⅞ in., D. of rim
8⅞ in., W. of rim 1⅛ in.
64.1625

250. Plate
Marks: A, twice, B, once. H. 1 in.,
D. of rim 9⅜ in., W. of rim 1¼ in.
Gift of the sons of the late Francis
H. Bigelow. 43.91

Timothy Boardman
& Company
(Timothy Boardman,
1798-1825)
New York City, active 1822-
1825
251. Beaker*
Mark: A, outside bottom. H. 5⅛
in., D. of rim 3½ in., D. of base
2¾ in.
64.1710

252. Beaker
Mark: A, outside bottom. H. 5⅛
in., D. of rim 3½ in., D. of base
2⅞ in.
64.1711

253. Beaker
Mark: A, outside bottom. H. 5⅛
in., D. of rim 3½ in., D. of base
2⅞ in.
64.2333

254. Beaker
Mark: A, outside bottom. H. 5⅛
in., D. of rim 3½ in., D. of base
2⅞ in.
64.2334

Boardman & Hart
(T. D. & S. Boardman
& Lucius Hart)
New York City, active 1828-
1853
255. Teapot*
Marks: B, C, outside bottom.
H. 8⅝ in.
64.1769

256. Beaker*
Marks: B, C, outside bottom.
H. 5⅛ in., D. of rim 3½ in., D. of
base 2⅞ in.
64.1708

257. Plate*
Marks: A, twice, B, C, once.
H. ⅞ in., D. of rim 9⅜ in., W. of
rim 1⅛ in.
Purchased of F. H. Bigelow. 14.930

258. Beaker
Marks: B, C. H. 3⅛ in., D. of rim
2⅞ in., D. of base 2⅛ in.
64.2332

259. Plate
Marks: B, C. H. ⅞ in., D. of rim
8⅞ in., W. of rim 1¼ in.
64.1627

260. Plate
Marks: B, C. H. ½ in., D. of rim
7¾ in., W. of rim 1 in.
64.2280

261. Plate
Mark: D. H. ⅞ in., D. of rim
9⅜ in., W. of rim 1¼ in.
64.2281

262. Plate
Marks: B, C. H. ⅝ in., D. of rim
7¾ in., W. of rim 1 in.
64.2282

Timothy Brigden
1774-1819
Albany, New York, active
1816-1819

263. Chalice*
Mark: A, bottom of bowl and
inside base. H. 9 in., D. of rim 4 in.,
D. of base 4½ in.
64.1742

Ephraim Capen
&
George Molineux
New York City, active 1848-1854

264. Nursing or sparkling lamp*
Mark: A, outside bottom. H. 2⅞ in.
64.1826

265. Lamp
Mark: A, outside bottom. H. 2⅛ in.
64.1827

Daniel Curtiss
1799/1800-1872

Albany, New York, active
1822-1840

266. Cuspidor*
Mark: B, inside base. H. 3¼ in.,
D. of rim 5¾ in., D. of base 4½ in.
64.1874

267. Deep dish
Mark: A, twice. H. 1⅜ in., D. of
rim 11⅛ in., W. of rim 1¼ in.
64.1681

268. Dish
Mark: A, twice. H. 1⅜ in., D. of
rim 11 in., W. of rim 1¼ in.
64.2311

William Ellsworth
1746-1816
New York City, active 1767-
1798
Mark refs.: A. LIL, vol. 2, 506;
CFM, p. 221. B. LIL, vol. 2, 505;
CFM, p. 221.
Marks:
A Not illustrated
B

269. Plate
Marks: A, twice, B, once. H. ⅝ in.,
D. of rim 8⅞ in., W. of rim 1 in.
64.2364

Edmund Endicott
&
William F. Sumner
New York City, active 1746-
1851

270. Lamp*
Marks: A, B, outside bottom.
H 3¾ in.
64.1829

Gaius Fenn
&
Jason Fenn
New York City, active 1831-
1843

271. Inkwell*
Mark: A, outside bottom. H. 1¾

in., D. of rim 2½ in., D. of base
2½ in.
64.1871

Henry Hopper
New York City, active 1842-
1847

272. Pair of candlesticks with
inserts*
Mark: A, outside bottom.
H. 10⅛ in.
64.1815a, b; 64.1816a, b

273. Ladle*
Mark: A, underside of handle top.
L. 13¼ in., D. of bowl 3⅞ in.
64.1878

274. Candlestick with insert
Mark: A, outside bottom.
H. 10⅛ in.
64.1817a, b

Charles Ostrander
&
George Norris
New York City, active 1848-
1850

275. Saucer candlestick with insert*
Mark: A, outside bottom.
H. 5¼ in.
64.1820a, b

276. Candlestick with insert
Mark: A, outside bottom.
H. 9⅞ in.
64.1819a, b

Renton & Company
New York City, active 1830's

277. Lamp*
Mark: A, outside bottom.
H. 2⅛ in.
64.1832

Spencer Stafford
1772-1844
Albany, New York, active
ca. 1820-1827

278. Deep dish*
Marks: B, C. H. 1⅜ in., D. of rim
13½ in., W. of rim 1⅝ in.
64.1688

279. Plate
Marks: A, B. H. ⅞ in., D. of rim
8¾ in., W. of rim 1⅛ in.
64.1665

James Weekes
New York City, active 1820-1835

280. Beaker*
Mark: A, outside bottom. H. 3⅛ in., D. of rim 2⅞ in., D. of base 2⅛ in.
64.1717

281. Beaker
Mark: A, outside bottom. H. 3⅛ in., D. of rim 3 in., D. of base 2⅛ in.
64.1718

282. Beaker
Mark: A, outside bottom. H. 3¼ in., D. of rim 2¾ in., D. of base 2 in.
64.1719

Thomas Wildes
New York City, active 1833-1840

283. Pair of candlesticks with inserts
Mark: A, outside bottom. H. 10 in.
64.1823a, b; 64.1824a, b

284. Saucer lamp*
Mark: A, outside bottom.
H. 4⅛ in.
64.1838

Henry Will
ca. 1735-ca. 1802
New York City, active 1761-1775, 1783-1793; Albany, New York, active 1776-1783

285. Basin*
Mark: A, inside bottom. H. 1⅞ in., D. 8 in., W. of rim ⅜ in.
64.1706

286. Quart tankard*
Mark: B, inside bottom. H. 6⅞ in., D. of rim 4⅜ in., D. of base 4⅞ in.
64.1741

Henry Yale
&
Stephen Curtis
New York City, active 1858-1867
Mark refs.: A. LIL, vol. 2, p. 118; CFM, p. 229.

Mark:
A

287. Lamp
Mark: A, outside bottom.
H. 8½ in.
64.1839

Peter Young
1749-1813
New York City, active 1775-1785; Albany, New York, active 1785-1795

288. Chalice*
Mark: A, outside base. H. 8½ in., D. of rim 4 in., D. of base 4⅜ in.
64.1743

Pennsylvania

Blakeslee Barns
1781-1823
Philadelphia, Pennsylvania, active 1812-1817

289. Deep dish*
Mark: A. H. 1⅜ in., D. of rim 11⅛ in., W. of rim 1¼ in.
64.1676

290. Dish
Marks: A, B. H. 1⅜ in., D. of rim 11⅛ in., W. of rim 1¼ in.
64.1677

291. Plate
Mark: A. H. 1 in., D. of rim 7⅞ in., W. of rim 1 in.
64.1615

292. Basin
Mark: A, inside bottom. H. 1½ in., D. of rim 6½ in., W. of rim ⅜ in.
64.1693

Parks Boyd
1771/2-1819
Philadelphia, Pennsylvania, 1795-1819

293. Pint mug*
Mark: B, inside bottom. H. 4⅛ in., D. of rim 3¼ in., D. of base 3⅞ in.
64.1722

294. Teapot*
Mark: B, inside bottom. H. 6 in.
64.1795

295. Plate
Mark: B. H. ⅜ in., D. of rim 7⅞ in., W. of rim 1⅛ in.
64.1628

296. Plate
Mark: A. H. ⅝ in., D. of rim 7⅞ in., W. of rim 1⅛ in.
64.1629

Simon Edgell
d. 1742
Philadelphia, Pennsylvania, active 1713-1742
Mark refs.: A. LIL, vol. 2, 527; CFM, p. 221. B. LIL, vol. 2, 528; CFM, p. 221. C. LIL, vol. 2, 529; CFM, p. 221.

Marks:

A

B

C

297. Plate
Marks: A, B, C. H. ¾ in., D. of rim
9¼ in., W. of rim 1⅛ in.
64.1643

Benjamin Harbeson
ca. 1763-1824
&
Joseph Harbeson
1770-1822
Philadelphia, Pennsylvania,
active 1793-1803
Mark refs.: A. LIL, vol. 2, 549.
Mark:
A

298. Plate
Mark: A. H. ⅝ in., D. of rim 7⅞ in.,
W. of rim 1⅛ in.
64.1648

Louis Kruiger
Philadelphia, Pennsylvania,
active 1830's
299. Ladle*
Mark: A, underside of handle top.
L. 13½ in., D. of bowl 3⅜ in.
64.1888

William McQuilkin
Philadelphia, Pennsylvania,

active 1839-1853
300. Water pitcher*
Mark: A, outside bottom. H. 12 in.
64.1810

John H. Palethorp
&
Robert Palethorp, Jr.
1797-1822
Philadelphia, Pennsylvania,
active separately and in
partnership 1817-1845
301. Plate*
Mark: B. H. ½ in., D. of rim 7¾
in., W. of rim 1⅛ in.
64.1659
302. Beaker*
Mark: C, inside bottom. H. 3⅛ in.,
D. of rim 2⅞ in., D. of base 2 in.
64.1716
303. Plate
Mark: A. H. ⅝ in., D. of rim 7¾
in., W. of rim 1⅛ in.
64.1658
304. Dish
Mark: B. H. 1½ in., D. 10⅞ in.,
W. of rim 1¼ in.
64.2320

William Will
1742-1798
Philadelphia, Pennsylvania,
active 1764-1798
305. Quart pot*
Mark: C, inside bottom. H. 5⅞ in.,
D. of rim 3⅞ in., D. of base 4¾ in.
64.1728
306. Basin*
Mark: D, inside bottom. H. 1⅜ in.,
D. of rim 6¼ in., W. of rim ¼ in.
64.1705
307. Plate
Marks: A, once, B, twice. H. ⅝ in.,
D. of rim 8⅜ in., W. of rim 1 in.
64.1669

Lorenzo L. Williams
Philadelphia, Pennsylvania,
active 1838-1842
308. Baptismal bowl*
Mark: A, outside bottom. H. 4⅝
in., D. of rim 6⅝ in., D. of base
4¼ in.
64.1858

Maryland
Samuel Kilbourn
ca. 1770-1839
Baltimore, Maryland, active
1814-1839
Mark ref.: A. LIL, vol. 2, 569.
Mark:
A

309. Plate
Mark: A. H. ⅞ in., D. of rim 9⅛
in., W. of rim 1⅛ in.
64.2292
310. Plate
Mark: A. H. ½ in., D. of rim 7¾
in., W. of rim 1⅛ in.
64.2291
311. Plate
Mark: A. H. ⅞ in., D. of rim 9¼ in.,
W. of rim 1⅛ in.
64.1651
312. Basin
Mark: A, inside bottom. H. 2¾ in.,
D. of rim 11⅞ in., W. of rim ⅜ in.
64.1700

George Lightner
1749-1815
Baltimore, Maryland, active
1806-1815
313. Plate*
Mark: A, twice. H. ½ in., D. of rim
7¾ in., W. of rim 1 in.
64.1655

Virginia

Joseph Danforth, Jr.
1783-1844
Richmond, Virginia, active
1807-1812
Mark refs.: A. LIL, vol. 1, 379;
CFM, p. 219. B. LIL, vol. 1, 380.
Marks:
A

B

314. Plate
Marks: A, B. H. ¾ in., D. of rim
8¾ in., W. of rim 1⅛ in.
64.2284

Unknown Makers

Unknown Maker
Mark attributed to Gershom
Jones
Providence, Rhode Island
Mark ref.: A. LIL, vol. 2, 600.
Mark:
A

315. Basin
Mark: A, inside bottom. H. 1⅞ in.,
D. of rim 7¾ in., W. of rim ⅜ in.
64.2331
316. Basin
Mark: A, inside bottom. H. 1⅞ in.,
D. of rim 7¾ in., W. of rim ⅜ in.
64.2330

Unknown Maker, "R. G."
Probably Boston, Massachusetts
Mark ref.: A. CFM, p. 150.
Mark:
A

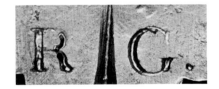

317. Porringer, crown handle
Mark: A, cast in handle bracket.
H. 1½ in., D. of rim 4⅛ in.
64.1752

Unknown Maker, "S. G."
Probably Boston, Massachusetts
Mark refs.: A. LIL, vol. 2, 574;
CFM, p. 150.
Mark:
A

318. Porringer, crown handle
Mark: A, cast in handle bracket.
H. 1¾ in., D. of rim 5¾ in.
64.1757

Unknown Maker, "I. C."
Probably Boston, Massachusetts
319. Porringer, crown handle*
Mark: A, cast in handle bracket.
H. 1⅝ in., D. of rim 4⅝ in.
64.1751

Unknown Maker, "E. C."
New York or New England
320. Porringer, "old English"
handle*
Mark: A, cast in handle bracket.
H. 1⅜ in., D. of rim 4½ in.
64.1750

Unknown Maker
Probably Newport, Rhode Island
321. Porringer, triangular handle*
No mark. "M E" stamped on handle top, owner or maker? H. 1⅝ in.,
D. of rim 5 in.
64.1764

Unknown Maker
Probably Hartford, Connecticut
322. Porringer, dolphin handle*
No mark. H. 1⅞ in., D. of rim
5¾ in.
64.1766

Unknown Maker
Probably New England
1800-1830
323. Porringer, heart-shaped
handle*
No mark. H. 1 in., D. of rim 3⅜ in.
64.1767

Unknown Maker
Probably Rhode Island or
Connecticut
324. Porringer, flower handle*
No mark. H. 1½ in., D. of rim
4¼ in.
64.1765

Unknown Maker, "T. S."
Possibly American, probably
English

325. Quart tankard, domed lid,
tulip form body*

Mark: A, inside bottom. H. 6 in.,
D. of rim 4⅛ in., D. of base 4½ in.
64.1740

Unknown Maker, "W. R."
Possibly American, probably
English

326. Quart tankard, domed lid,
tulip form body*
Mark: "W R" under a crown to left
of top handle joint (not illustrated).
H. 5⅞ in., D. of rim 4¼ in., D. of
base 4¾ in.
Gift of Mr. and Mrs. William
deForest Thomson. 19.553

Unknown Maker
Probably Newport, Rhode
Island, or Boston, Massachusetts,
ca. 1750-1775

327. Quart pot*
Mark: A, inside bottom. H. 5⅞ in.,
D. of rim 3⅞ in., D. of base 4¾ in.
Lent by Mrs. George A. Marks.
146.1972

Unknown Maker, "C. I."
Probably New England

328. Quart tankard, domed lid,
flared body*
Mark: "C I" cast in handle.
H. 6⅜ in., D. of rim 4⅛ in., D. of
base 4⅝ in.
64.1737

Unknown Maker
Probably New York

329. Quart tankard, flat lid*
No mark. H. 5⅜ in., D. of rim
4¼ in., D. of base 4¾ in.
64.1738

Unknown Maker

330. Fireman's trumpet*
No mark. L. 16¾ in., D. of horn
opening 7⅝ in.
64.1875

331. Ladle*
No mark. L. 14 in., D. of bowl
3¾ in.
64.1889

332. Egg tongs*
No mark. "1809" stamped on
handle side. L. 8 in.
64.1892

333. Cream pitcher*
No mark. H. 5⅞ in.
64.1808

334. Flagon with spout*
No mark. H. 10⅞ in., D. of rim
3¾ in., D. of base 6½ in.
64.1736

335. Lamp*
No mark. H. 11 in.
64.1842

336. Beaker*
No mark. Engraved "Keziah
Kimball/and/Isaac Felch/May 3,
1826." H. 3 in., D. of rim 3 in.,
D. of base 2¼ in.
64.2342

337. Spoon mold*
No mark. L. 7⅝ in. Ref.: LIL, vol.
3, 750, 751.
64.1886

338. Funnel*
No mark. H. 4 in., D. 3½ in.
Gift of Mr. and Mrs. William
deForest Thomson. 19.555

339. Teapot stand*
No mark. L. 6⅛ in.
64.1869

340. Salt*
No mark. H. 2½ in., D. of rim
2⅝ in., D. of base 2⅞ in.
Bequest of Bessie Paine Bigelow.
24.174

341. Teapot*
No mark. H. 6¼ in.
64.1791

342. Bullseye lamp*
No mark. "Patent" stamped on
lense holder top. H. 8½ in.
64.1840

343. Basin
No mark. H. 1⅞ in., D. of rim 6 in.,
W. of rim ¼ in.
64.1696

344. Beaker
Mark: a crown. H. 4⅛ in., D. of
rim 3⅞ in., D. of base 3⅞ in.
64.1720

345. Beaker
No mark. H. 3 in., D. of rim 3 in.,
D. of base 2¼ in.
64.1721

346. Beaker
No mark. H. 3½ in., D. of rim 3 in.,
D. of base 2 in.

Gift of the sons of the late Henry
Forbes Bigelow. 43.106

347. Beaker
No mark. H. 3½ in., D. of rim 3½
in., D. of base 2⅛ in.
Gifts of the sons of the late Henry
Forbes Bigelow. 43.107

348. Beaker
No mark. H. 3 in., D of rim 3 in.,
D. of base 2 in.
64.2340

349. Beaker
No mark. H. 2⅞ in., D. of rim 3 in.,
D. of base 2 in.
64.2341

350. Beaker
No mark. H. 2⅞ in., D. of rim
3 in., D. of base 2 in.
64.2337

351. Beaker
No mark. H. 2⅞ in., D. of rim 3 in.,
D. of base 2 in.
64.2338

352. Beaker
No mark. H. 2¾ in., D. of rim 2¾
in., D. of base 2¼ in.
64.2339

353. Beaker
No mark. H. 2½ in., D. of rim 2⅝
in., D. of base 2 in.
64.2343

354. Beaker
No mark. H. 2¾ in., D. of rim 2¾
in., D. of base 1⅞ in.
64.2344

356. Handled beaker, silvered
No mark. H. 4 in., D. of rim 3¼ in.,
D. of base 3 in.
64.2350

357. Handled beaker, silvered
No mark. H. 4⅛ in., D. of rim 3½
in., D. of base 3 in.
64.2351

358. Bowl
No mark. H. 2¼ in., D. of rim 5½
in., D. of base 3⅛ in.
Gift of the sons of the late Henry
Forbes Bigelow. 43.108

359. Bowl
No mark. H. 2¼ in., D. of rim 5½
in., D. of base 3⅛ in.
Gift of the sons of the late Henry
Forbes Bigelow. 43.109

360. Breast protector

No mark. H. 1½ in.
64.1890

361. Candlestick
No mark. H. 4¼ in.
Gift of Miss Catherine Waters
Faucon. 28.348

362. Chalice
No mark. H. 5¾ in., D. of rim
3⅜ in.
64.1744

363. Chalice and top plate
No mark. H. 4⅜ in., D. of rim
3½ in.
Gift of Sears B. Condit in memory
of Mary L. Condit. 47.191-192

364. Commode
No mark. H. 7¼ in., D. of rim
11¾ in.
64.1864

365. Cuspidor
No mark. H. 4⅜ in., D. of rim
9½ in.
64.1885

366. Dram bottle
No mark. H. 4¾ in.
64.1865

367. Flagon
No mark. H. 8½ in., D. of rim 3¾
in., D. of base 5 in.
Purchased of F. H. Bigelow. 14.927

368. Flagon
No mark. H. 11⅜ in., D. of rim
4 in., D. of base 5¾ in.
Purchased of F. H. Bigelow. 14.928

369. Funnel
No mark. L. 5⅞ in., D. of rim
4⅞ in.
64.1872

370. Ladle
Mark: "Ferré" stamped on bottom
of handle. L. 13⅝ in., D. of bowl
3¾ in.
64.1887

371. Ladle
No mark. L. 13½ in., D. of bowl
3⅝ in.
64.2367

372. Inkwell
No mark. H. 1¾ in., D. of rim
2⅝ in., D. of base 2⅞ in.
Gift of Mr. and Mrs. William
deForest Thomson. 19.547

373. Inkwell
No mark. H. 3 in., D. of rim 3 in.,

D. of base 4⅜ in.
Bequest of Bessie Paine Bigelow.
24.173

374. Inkwell
No mark. H. 3½ in., D. of rim 3¼
in., D. of base 3⅛ in.
Bequest of Bessie Paine Bigelow.
24.175

375. Inkwell
No mark. H. 3⅜ in., D. of rim 4¾
in., D. of base 2 in.
Gift of the sons of the late Henry
Forbes Bigelow. 43.110

376. Lamp
No mark. H. 3½ in.
Gift of Mr. and Mrs. William
deForest Thomson. 19.537

377. Lamp
No mark. H. 3⅝ in.
Gift of Mr. and Mrs. William
deForest Thomson. 19.538

378. Lamp
No mark. H. 5 in.
Gift of Mr. and Mrs. William
deForest Thomson. 19.539

379. Lamp
No mark. H. 6 in.
Gift of Mr. and Mrs. William
deForest Thomson. 19.540

380. Lamp
No mark. H. 6½ in.
Gift of Mr. and Mrs. William
deForest Thomson. 19.541

381. Bullseye lamps
No mark. H. 9⅞ in.
Bequest of Bessie Paine Bigelow.
24.177, 24.178

382. Bullseye lamp
No mark. "Patent" stamped on
lense top. H. 8¾ in.
64.1841, a, b, c

383. Lamp
No mark. H. 7¼ in.
64.1843

384. Lamp
No mark. H. 7¼ in.
64.1844

385. Ship's lamp
No mark. H. 4⅛ in.
64.1847

386. Lamp
No mark. 4⅞ in.
64.1845

387. Lamp
No mark. H. 4⅝ in.
64.1846

388. Lamp
No mark. H. 4⅛ in.
64.1848

389. Ship's lamp
No mark. H. 3⅞ in.
64.1849

390. Lamp
No mark. H. 3¾ in.
64.1850

391. Lamp
No mark. H. 4 in.
64.1852

392. Lamp
No mark. H. 3¼ in.
64.1854

393. Nursing or sparking lamp
No mark. H. 3¾ in.
64.1851

394. Nursing or sparking lamp
No mark. H. 3 in.
64.1853

395. Pap spoon
No mark. L. 5¼ in.
64.1879

396. Plate
No mark. H. ½ in., D. of rim
6⅛ in., W. of rim ⅝ in.
64.2304

397. Plate
No mark. H. ⅝ in., D. of rim 6 in.,
W. of rim ¾ in.
64.2305

398. Plate
No mark. H. ¼ in., D. of rim
5⅛ in., W. of rim ⅝ in.
64.1670

399. Plate
No mark. H. ½ in., D. of rim
5⅛ in., W. of rim ⅝ in.
64.1671

400. Plate
No mark. H. ⅝ in., D. of rim
12¼ in., W. of rim 1¾ in.
Gift of Mrs. Joseph Cushman.
Res. 60.5

401. Plate
No mark. H. ⅝ in., D. of rim
12¼ in., W. of rim 1¾ in.
Gift of Mrs. Joseph Cushman.
Res. 60.6

402. Porringer
No mark. Crown type handle.
H. 1¾ in., D. of rim 5¼ in.
64.1763

403. Quart measure
Mark: "VRC" beneath a crown,
at the rim. H. 6 in., D. of rim
4⅛ in., D. of base 4½ in.
Gift of Mr. and Mrs. William
deForest Thomson. 19.552

404. Spoon mold
No mark. L. 8¼ in.
Bequest of Charles Hitchcock Tyler.
32.353

405. Syringe
No mark. L. 11⅞ in., D. of cylinder
1½ in.
64.2368

406. Syringe
No mark. L. 11¾ in., D. of cylinder
2 in.
64.2372

407. Syringe
No mark. L. 14¼ in., D. of cylinder
1⅞ in.
64.1891

408. Syrup jug
No mark. H. 5⅞ in.
64.1805

409. Teapot
No mark. H. 10 in.
64.1791

410. Teapot
No mark. H. 8½ in.
64.1792

411. Water pitcher
No mark. H. 7⅝ in.
64.1809

Selected Bibliography

"American Pewter, Garvan and Other Collections at Yale." *Yale University Art Gallery Bulletin.* Fall 1965.

The Bulletin of the Pewter Collectors' Club of America, published semiannually since 1934.

Cotterell, Howard Herschel. *Old Pewter, Its Makers and Marks.* London: B. T. Batsford Ltd., 1929.

de Jonge, Eric. "Johann Christoph Heyne, Pewterer, Minister, Teacher." *Winterthur Portfolio 4.* Winterthur, Delaware: The Henry Francis du Pont Winterthur Museum, 1968, pp. 169-184.

Goyne, Nancy A. "Britannia in America: The Introduction of a New Alloy and a New Industry." *Winterthur Portfolio 2.* Winterthur, Delaware: The Henry Francis du Pont Winterthur Museum, 1965, pp. 160-196.

Hamilton, Suzanne C. "The Pewter of William Will: A Checklist." *Winterthur Portfolio 7.* Winterthur, Delaware: The Henry Francis du Pont Winterthur Museum, 1972, pp. 129-160.

Jacobs, Carl. *Guide to American Pewter.* New York: The McBride Company, 1957.

Kerfoot, John Barrett. *American Pewter.* Boston: Houghton Mifflin Company, 1924.

Laughlin, Ledlie Irwin. *Pewter in America: Its Makers and Their Marks.* 2 volumes. Boston: Houghton Mifflin Company, 1940; volume 3. Barre, Massachusetts: Barre Publishers, 1971.

Montgomery, Charles F. *A History of American Pewter.* A Winterthur Book. New York: Praeger, 1973.

Pewter in America 1650-1900, an Exhibition. Manchester, New Hampshire: The Currier Gallery of Art, 1968.